THE HEPTNER SISTERS

WYOMING SCHOOL TEACHERS

Compiled by
Lorna Jean Whisler
119 Homeaway Lane
Natural Bridge, Virginia
2018

Cover and print book interior design
by Theresa Marie Flaherty

Turas Publishing
4833 Saratoga Blvd., No. 129
Corpus Christi, TX 78413

www.TurasPublishing.com

ISBN: 978-0-9982215-0-2

TURAS
PUBLISHING

Jeanette Louise and Leona Sophia Heptner
(1925)

In memory of

Laura Margarete (Young) Heptner,
Grandma Heptner, the 1st

and

for her Great Grandchildren

Jerry, Bruce, Merlyn, Kim,
Mary Kay, DeeDe (deceased), Corina,
Randy, and Marleen

Who are now grandparents themselves

TABLE OF CONTENTS

INTRODUCTION

This is a history of two extraordinary ordinary people. Leona and Jeanette Heptner, who were first sisters, and secondly Wyoming school teachers. Leona, born August 2, 1912, in Glenwood, Mills County, Iowa, was almost two years old when she arrived on an immigrant train with her mother, her older sister Irene, and two brothers, Eugene and Oscar, on May 31, 1914, at Moorcroft, Crook County, Wyoming. Her father met them with a team and wagon to bring them to the homestead he had filed on in 1913. He had come earlier on an immigrant train bringing a cow, two horses, Fanny and Red, and a mule named Jenny, and various farming equipment with him. Jeanette was born March 1, 1920, at home on the family homestead about nine miles north of Rozet located in the community called Little Iowa.

Leona and Jeanette grew up on the family homestead, attending grade school at the Cottonwood rural school (later known as the Woods School) and Rozet Consolidated school. Leona graduated from Rozet High School in May 1930 and Jeanette graduated from Campbell County High School in May 1939. After attending Normal Training at Campbell County High School in 1930-1931, Leona taught all her teaching years in Campbell County, Wyoming, except for one school term in Crook County. Jeanette, upon completing Normal Training in 1939-1940, also taught in rural schools in Campbell and Crook Counties, plus schools in Big Horn and Weston counties. Both graduated with Bachelor of Arts degrees in Education from the University of Wyoming, Jeanette on June 4, 1951, and Leona on August 21, 1953. On July 29, 1960, Jeanette received her Master of Science degree in Education from the Nebraska State Teachers College in Chadron, Nebraska.

This book will not only focus on the schools in which they taught, but also on the history of their ancestors and their immediate family, reflecting their early years on the family homestead located north of Rozet.

PART ONE

THEIR

IMMIGRANT ANCESTORS

ANTON HEPTNER (1844-1927)
and
MARY EBERHARDT (1851-1900)

Anton Heptner

Mary Eberhardt

Anton and Mary were the parents of Frank Herman Heptner who homesteaded north of Rozet in 1913. Anton's date of birth, as provided by his daughters, was September 29, 1844, in Prussia. No record for date of birth, other than family tradition has been found. The 1900 Federal Census record for Anton finds him listed as a widower and his family living in Walker Township, Moniteau County, Missouri. It also indicates Anton immigrated to the United States in 1872. It is likely that he immigrated to the United States to escape the political upheaval that was occurring in Prussia at that time. Neither his immigration nor his naturalization records have yet been located. Marriage record recently found for Anton and Mary Eberhardt tells us they were married on March 23, 1876, in Moniteau County, Missouri.

Anton and Mary are found in the 1880 Federal Census Schedule taken on June 10, 1880; where his occupation was listed as a farmer in the township of Marion, Cole County, Missouri, which borders Moniteau County. His family at that time consisted of: his wife, Mary, age 29, born in Ohio; son Otto, age 10; son Frank, age 3, daughter Minnie, age 2, and son Walter, age 9 months. Each of the children was listed as having been born in Missouri to parents born in Prussia and Ohio. However, if Anton immigrated to this country in 1872 as the 1900 census indicates, then Otto who was born on July 22, 1870, would have been born in Prussia. In this case, Anton would have been married in Prussia and immigrated to the United States with possibly his wife and his son Otto. No records have been found substantiating this theory.

Mary Eberhardt, daughter of Nicholas and Elizabeth (Hagi) Eberhardt, was born on December 15, 1851 in Warwick, Tuscarawas County, Ohio. In reviewing Census Records, it is believed that her parents had stopped there for about a year on their way to Missouri from Worb, Canton Berne, Switzerland. Mary Eberhardt Heptner died March 28, 1900, near California, Moniteau County, Missouri, from a buggy accident according to correspondence in the 1970s with her daughters. She and her two-year-old daughter, Emma, are buried in Crown Hill Cemetery, California, Moniteau County, Missouri. At the time of her death her youngest child, Ella, was five years old.

The 1900 Federal Census Schedule shows Anton living in Moniteau County, Missouri, a widower with four daughters: Minnie, age 22; Anna, age 19; Leona, age 17; Clara, age 12; and one son, Walter, age 20. His youngest daughter Lena was not listed. The conjecture is that she may have been visiting her grandparents, Nicholas and Elizabeth (Hagi) Eberhardt, on that day. Anton's oldest son, Otto, was found living in Moreau Township, Cole County, Missouri, with his first wife, Rosa, and three children, Walter, age 6, Eddie, age 4, and Mary, age two months. No record was found in the 1900 census records for Frank Heptner. He may have already moved out of Missouri at that time. He eventually moved to Mills County, Iowa, where he was married in 1904.

Records reviewed reflect that the children of Anton and Mary were born in Cole County and Moniteau County, Missouri, as follows:

Otto Daniel	born July 22, 1870 in Russellville, Cole County, Missouri, married 1st, Rosa Wilson, 2nd Della Defoe;
Frank Herman	**born December 6, 1876, at Russellville, Cole County, Missouri, married Laura Young in Mills County, Iowa;**
Wilhelmina *Minnie*	born March 20, 1878, at Russellville, Cole County, Missouri, married Samuel Eugene Archer;
Walter Benjamin	born September 1, 1878, at Russellville, Cole County, Missouri, died January 29, 1911 at Visalia, Tulare County, California, never married;
Anna Elizabeth	born March 13, 1882, at Russellville, Cole County, Missouri, never married;
Lena Louise	born March 13, 1883, at Russellville, Cole County; Missouri, married John Thomas Wilson;
Emma	born February 13, 1887, at Russellville, Cole County, Missouri, died March 28, 1889, at McGirk, Moniteau County, Missouri;
Clara Leona	born May 24, 1888, at McGirk, Moniteau County, Missouri, married Harry E. Aulman;
John Fredrick	born December 15, 1889, at McGirk, Moniteau County, Missouri, married Nora May Clore;
Mary Alma	born November 22, 1891, at McGirk, Moniteau County, Missouri, who married Carl D. Cooper;
Ella Gertrude	born January 24, 1894, at McGirk, Moniteau County, Missouri, and married Harry Lacrosse.

Anton Heptner moved to Visalia, Tulare County, California, about 1904 where he continued to pursue farming as an occupation. All his children, except Frank, went with him. There they married and continued to live in or near Visalia, California, for the rest of their lives. Anton died August 22, 1927 in Visalia, California. He is buried in the Visalia City Cemetery, Visalia, California.

CHILDREN OF ANTON and Mary (Eberhardt) HEPTNER

Otto Daniel
(1870-1946)

Frank Herman
(1876-1928)

Wilhelmina
(1877-1964)

Walter Benjamin
(1878-1911)

Anna Elizabeth
(1882-1973)

Lena Louise
(1883-1972)

Clara Leona
(1888-1983)

John Fredrick
(1889-1941)

Ella Gertrude   Mary Alma
(1894-1977)   (1891-1980)

State of Missouri
County of Moniteau

I do hereby certify, That on twenty third (23) day of March 1876, personally appeared before me, Mr. Anton Hefner and Miss. Mary Eberhard both of this county, who were with their mutual consent lawfully joined together in Holy Matrimony, which was solemnized by me,

F. A. Umbeck
w. Pastor

Filed May 20" 1876,

Wm, G, Howe and Recorder,

Marriage Certificate for Anton Heptner and Mary Eberhardt
Copied from the Moniteau County 1876 Marriage Records, California, Missouri, USA

Lena (Heptner) Wilson, Ella (Heptner) LaCrosse,
Minnie (Heptner) Archer, Annie Heptner
Visalia, Tulare County, California
About 1953

JOHN EBERHARDT (1795-1875)
and
BARBARA STOLL (1794-1870)

Both **John and Barbara Anne (Stoll) Eberhardt** were born in the Canton Berne, Switzerland, John about 1795, and Barbara about 1794. His occupation was that of a farmer. He was approximately 50 years of age when they immigrated to the United States from Switzerland, with their children. They arrived in the United States on May 18, 1845 and settled near Warwick, Tuscarawas County, Ohio, where they appeared on the 1850 Federal Census Schedule. John and Barbara were the parents of six children:

Jacob	born about 1820, in Canton Berne, Switzerland;
Nicholas	**born about 1823, in Canton Berne, Switzerland, married Elizabeth Hagi;**
Anna	born about 1828, in Canton Berne Switzerland;
Elizabeth	born March 25, 1831, in Berne Switzerland, married Frederick Messerly;
Benedick	born October 3, 1833, in Canton Berne, Switzerland, married Catherine Dahl;
Johannes	born 1835; died April 23, 1835, in Canton Berne, Switzerland; and
Frederick	born July 11, 1840, in Canton Berne, Switzerland, married Rosanna Messerly.

In 1860 John and Barbara traveled down the Ohio and Mississippi Rivers to Moniteau County, Missouri, where he established a farm. John died in February 1875 at California, Moniteau County, Missouri. Barbara died January 22, 1870 at California, Moniteau County, Missouri.

NICHOLAS EBERHARDT (1823-1907)
and
ELIZABETH HAGI (1830-1924)

Nicholas Eberhardt, John and Barbara's second son married **Elizabeth Hagi** about 1851 in Warwick, Tuscarawas County, Ohio. She was a daughter of Benedict Hagi. She was born August 12, 1830, at Worb, Canton Berne, Switzerland. When they immigrated to America is not known. They are found living in Tuscarawas County, Ohio, in 1850. Nicholas and Elizabeth were the parents of seven known children:

Mary	**born on December 15, 1851 in Warwick, Tuscarawas County, Ohio, married Anton Heptner;**
Frank E.	born in 1853, at Warwick, Tuscarawas County, Ohio, married Mary Cramer; and
John Henry	date and place of birth unknown, possibly in Warwick, Tuscarawas County, Ohio, married Mary Ann Early.

At some point between 1853 and 1864 Nicholas moved his family to California, Moniteau County, Missouri, where their younger children were born:

Anna	born December 17, 1864, California, Moniteau County, Missouri, never married;
Lena	born August 30, 1866, California, Moniteau County, Missouri, married Frank John Isenhart;
Daniel	born May 13, 1871, California, Moniteau County, Missouri, never married; and
William	born July 16, 1876, California, Moniteau County, Missouri.

Nicholas enlisted in Company H, Provisional Missouri Militia, in Moniteau County, in September 1865, serving in the last days of the Civil War. Nicholas died April 22, 1907, and Elizabeth (Hagi) Eberhardt died May 26, 1924, in California, Moniteau County, Missouri. Both are buried in the Evangelical Cemetery, California, Moniteau County, Missouri.

ELIZABETH (HAGI) EBERHARDT
(1830-1924)

Immigrated about 1849/50 from Worb, Canton Berne, Switzerland, possibly with her
father Benedick Hagi, to Tuscarawas County, Ohio.
She married Nicholas Eberhardt about 1850 in Tuscarawas County, Ohio

JACOB, YOUNG, SR. (1818-1884)
and
SAHRA SALOMEA (SIMON) YOUNG (1819-1903)

Jacob Young, Sr. and Sahra Salomea (Simon) Young were both born in Alsace, Germany. Jacob was born, April 3, 1818. Salomea was born, October 1, 1818/19 at Engweiler, Alsace, Germany, according to her death record in the Salem Church records, Plummer Settlement, Mills County, Iowa. These records are now held at the Lutheran Church of Trayner, Iowa. Six children were born to them in Alsace. Their two oldest sons, Jacob and Hans, died young. About 1850-53, Jacob and Salomea with their four or five children immigrated to the United States. Their first stop was at Loudonville, Ashland County, Ohio, where their youngest child, John, was born January 21, 1854. Land Deed Records for Pottawattamie County, Iowa, reflect that a Jacob Young purchased forty acres from William Hart. It also indicates that he bought forty acres from J. H. Plummer in 1851. All indications show that the family was not in Pottawattamie County by 1851, but it is possible that he may have gone ahead to look for lands while his family was temporarily living in Ashland County, Ohio. However, this is pure speculation now. Immigration and naturalization records for Jacob Young, Sr. and his family have not yet been located. Jacob and Salomea Young were the parents of eight children:

Jacob	born in Alsace, Germany and died young in Alsace;
Hans	born in Alsace, Germany and died young in Alsace;
Catherine	born in Alsace, Germany, and died at Loudenville, Ashland County, Ohio;
Sarah Salomea	born April 27, 1845, in Alsace, Germany, married Christian Henry Beck;
Jacob, Jr.	**born August 11, 1847, in Alsace, Germany, married Anna Marie Christina Fredericka Reinert;**
George	born October 17, 1849, in Alsace, Germany, married Katherine Harms;
Margaret	born November 22, 1852 in Alsace, Germany, or Ashland Co, Ohio, married Adolph Geise; and
John	born January 21, 1854, in Loudonville, Ashland, Ohio, married Matilda E. Reinert (sister of Freida).

After moving his family to Pottawattamie County, Iowa, Jacob took up farming on the land he had purchased. This land is in a lovely valley directly across the Missouri River from Omaha, Nebraska. The farm included rich bottomland along the Iowa side, which was planted in corn. Jacob Young, Sr. died October 9, 1884, and Salomea died January 25, 1903. They are both buried in the Salem Church Cemetery, in the Plummer Settlement, Pottawattamie County, Iowa. This church is no longer a functioning church but each year, over Memorial Day, the community organizes a homecoming celebration for the descendants of the families who were members of that church and those buried in the Salem Church Cemetery.

Sahra Salomea (Simon) Young
(1818-1903)
Laura (Young) Heptner's Grandmother

CHILDREN OF

JACOB, SR. and SAHRA SALOMEA (SIMON) YOUNG

Sarah Salomea
(1845-1922)

Jacob, Jr
(1847-1888)

George
(1849-1916)

Margaret
(1852-1900)

John
(1854-1940)

1903.

1 Salomea Young, geb. Simon, geb. am
1. Oktober 1819 zu Engweiler in Elsas
gest am 25. Januar 1903 zu Plummer Settlement
begraben am   Jan. auf dem Friedhof Hoff
Plummer Salems Kirche.

Copied from the Plummer Salem Church, 1903 death record for Sahra Salomea (Simon) Young

GERHARDT REINERT (1818-1876)
and
LOUISE BUSCHENFELDT (1830-1892)

Gerhardt Reinert was born November 25, 1818, in Germany. He immigrated to Moniteau County, Missouri, before January 1852. No record has been found for his marriage to Louise Buschenfeld, the daughter of Christopher Buschenfeld and Louise Campmeyer. It probably took place in Moniteau County, Missouri. Louise was born March 17, 1830, in Germany. No record of her parents has been located at this time. Sometime between 1854 and 1866 Gerhardt and Louise, with their five children, emigrated from Moniteau County, Missouri, to Pottawattamie County, Iowa.

Gerhardt and Louise Reinert were the parents of nine children, all but their youngest, were born in California, Moniteau County, Missouri. They are:

Ana Marie	born January 4, 1852, in Moniteau County, Missouri, married Ernest Kreft;
Anna Marie Christina Fredericka	**born January 18, 1854, in Moniteau County, Missouri, married Jacob Young, Jr;**
August	born January 5, 1856, in Moniteau County, Missouri, married Frieda Reischenback;
Matilda Emma	born December 20, 1858, in Moniteau County, Missouri, married John Young (brother of Jacob, Jr.);
Julius Wilhelm	born December 11, 1859, in Moniteau County, Missouri; never married;
Sophia	born in 1862, in Moniteau County, Missouri, married Wilhelm Schmiedeskamp;
Bertha	born November 20, 1866, in Mills County, Iowa, married John Fritz;
Christine Matilda Ida	born December 29, 1870, in Mills County, Iowa, married William Scheel; and
Christopher Gerhardt	born December 2, 1875, at Glenwood, Mills County, Iowa, married Emma Sophia Meyer.

The marriages of all above children can be found recorded in the Kirchbook of the St Paul's United Church, Dumphries, Pottawattaime County, Iowa. They lived their lives in or near Mills County, Iowa.

Gerhardt Reinert died November 15, 1876, at Glenwood, Mills County, Iowa. Louise Reinert died March 6, 1892, at Glenwood, Mills County, Iowa. They are both buried at St. Paul's United Christian Church, Dumphries, Pottawattamie County, Iowa.

Jacob Young, Jr. and Friedricka *Frieda* Reinert
Laura (Young) Heptner's Parents
1865
Frieda's parents, Gerhardt and Louise (Buschenfeld) Reinert,
immigrated to the United States about 1850 from Germany. They
settled for a time near California, Moniteau County, Missouri, about
the same time as the Heptner and Eberhardt families. The
Reinert family emigrated from Missouri to Mills County, Iowa, about 1865.

Jacob Young, Jr. (1847-1888)
and
Anna Marie Christine Friedricka *Frieda* Reinert (1853-1914)

Jacob Young, Jr. and Anna Marie Christine Fredericka *Freida* Reinert, daughter of Gerhardt and Louise (Buschenfeld) Reinert, were married on February 8, 1872. Their marriage was the first performed in a newly established St. Paul's United Church of Christ, Dumphries, Pottawattamie County, Iowa. Jacob and Frieda were the parents of nine children, all born in Mills County, Iowa:

Johann *John* Heinrich	born May 19, 1873, married Anna Basch;
Louise Matilda Ida	born September 13, 1874, married William Meppin;
Salomea Fredricka Sophia	born September 24, 1876, married Christopher Green;
Maria Fredericka Lydia	born January 5, 1879, married Herman Basch;
Julius Jacob	born May 30, 1881, died July 29, 1881;
George Gustov	born May 30, 1882, died August 29, 1882;
Laura Margarete	**born October 29, 1883, married Frank Herman Heptner;**
Herman August	born January 13, 1886, married Martha Boehm; and
Emma Sarah Elizabeth	born January 20, 1888, married Herman W. Boehm.

Except for their daughter, Laura, each of the above children grew up, married, lived, and died in Mills County, or surrounding counties all their lives. Many of their descendants live there today.

Jacob, Jr. died August 15, 1888, seven months after the birth of his last child Emma. Frieda continued living on the farm. She built the large framed white farmhouse that her relatives from Wyoming remember when they visited Iowa. The records of her purchases were saved and copied by her grandson, Arnim Young. The house had beautiful cherry wood moldings around each window and door. Frieda died on May 13, 1914. Two weeks later her daughter, Laura, and her children boarded an emigrant train for Rozet, Campbell County, Wyoming, to join her husband, Frank, who had gone to Wyoming in 1913. He homesteaded nine miles north of Rozet, Campbell County, Wyoming. Both Jacob and Frieda are buried in the churchyard of St. Paul's United Christian Church, Dumphries, Iowa.

The House that Freida Built

CHILDREN OF JACOB, JR. and FRIEDA (REINERT) YOUNG

Johann Heinrich
(1873-1957)

Louise Matilda Ida
(1974-1957)

Salomea Fredericka Sophia
(1876-1934)

Maria Fredericka Lydia
(1879-1958)

Laura Margarete
(1883-1950)

Herman August
(1886-1963)

Emma Sarah Elizabeth
(1888-1953)

Jacob Young, Jr. and Fredricka Young
Their wedding was the first performed at
St. Paul's United Christian Church, Dumfries, Pottawattaime County, Iowa
February 8, 1872

St. Paul's United Christian Church, Dumfries, Iowa
Established 1872

The graves of Jacob and Freida and their infant sons, Julius and George
are in the foreground, second row (1st 3 graves from the left).

FRIEDA (REINERT) YOUNG's FAMILY – about 1893
Glenwood, Mills County, Iowa
Back row: Louise Young, John Young, Lydia Young, Willie Bonne
Front Row: Emma Young, Friedricka *Frieda* Young (sitting),
Herman Young, Laura Young, Sophia Young

COMMUNICANT'S CLASS SEPTEMBER 1898
St. Paul's United Christian Church, Dumfries, Pottawattaime County, Iowa

Members: Standing: Lydia Young, John Young, and Laura Young
                         Sitting: (Names unknown, probably some were cousins)
                                 (St. Paul's Kirchbook, page 265, #587)

Johann H. Young and Anna Basch Wedding
February 22, 1900
Attendants – Johann Basch and Herman Meier
Lydia Young and Laura Young
St. Paul's United Christian Church, Dumfries, Pottawattaime County, Iowa

1894
Standing: Herman, Lydia, Laura, and
Sitting: Emma Young

About 1898
Lydia Young and Laura Young

Laura Margarete Young
January 22, 1900

PART TWO

THE HEPTNER FAMILY OF ROZET, CAMPBELL COUNTY, WYOMING

FRANK HERMAN HEPTNER (1876-1928)
and
LAURA MARGARETE YOUNG (1883-1950)

Frank Herman Heptner

Laura Margarete Young

Frank and Laura were married
on April 14, 1904
at
St. Paul's United Christian Church, Dumphries, Pottawattaime County, Iowa

(Copied from the Kirchbook of
St. Paul's United Christian Church, Dumfries, Pottawattaime County, Iowa)

THE CHILDREN OF FRANK and LAURA (YOUNG) HEPTNER

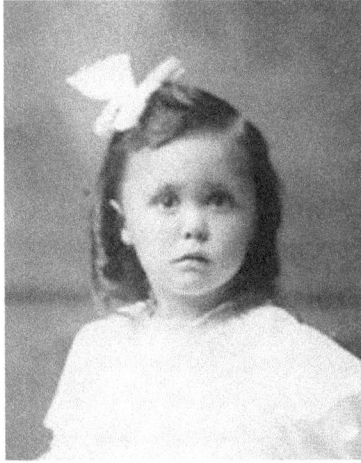

Olivia Anna Marie *Olive*
(1904-1907)

Irene Lydia Mina
(1906-1983)

Eugene John Anton
(1908-1979)

Oscar Herman
(1910-1977)

Leona Sophia
(1912-2001)

Wallace Edwin
(1918-1919)

Jeanette Louise
(1920-2002)

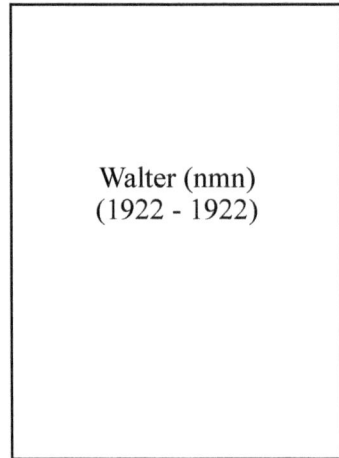

Walter (nmn)
(1922 - 1922)

(Lived only hours)

St. Paul's United Christian Church
Dumphries, Pottawattaime County, Iowa
(Established 1872)

It has been determined that Frank Heptner migrated from Moniteau County, Missouri, to Mills County, Iowa, between 1900 and 1904. Why he did not accompany his parents and his younger brothers and sisters to California will always provide fuel for "speculation." Marriage records indicate he was in Mills County, Iowa, before 1904 as he married Laura Margarete Young on April 14, 1904, in St. Paul's United Christian Church, Dumphries, Pottawattaime County, Iowa. The family lived in Mills County, Iowa. The Kirchbook for St. Paul's United Kirch records their marriage and the birth of their first five children:

Olivia Anna Maria *Olive*	born on May 4, 1904. She died December 21, 1907 and was buried in the church cemetery on December 23, 1907 at age 3 years and 7 months;
Irene Lydia Mina	born on May 31, 1906;
Eugene Johann Anton	born on February 29, 1908;
Oscar Herman	born on July 31, 1910; and
Leona Sophia	born on August 2, 1912.

Frank and Laura rented a farm near her parents, Jacob and Frieda Young, in Glenwood, Mills County, Iowa. Jeanette remembers her mother telling a story about her little boy, Eugene. It was about 1912 and she noticed Eugene stumbling around outside her window. His legs were not holding him up. He kept falling. He managed to walk to the garden and began to pull up carrots and radishes. His mother had a premonition; she went to the table and saw that the pitcher holding grape wine was empty! She understood then the reason for her little son's unsteady feet.

Another story Laura related to her children involved a young man who stopped at their house in Iowa and asked for something to eat. Frank told Laura to fix a pan of baking powder biscuits for him. Laura's biscuits were very good and delicious. The man began to eat with much vigor and enjoyment until he was filled. Frank saw him start to put his knife and fork down. Frank walked over and took his rifle down from the wall, sat down, and put the rifle across his knees. He looked at the man and said, "Eat more!" The man continued to eat. When all the biscuits were gone the man went on his way, very well fed.

Frank Heptner, holding Oscar, Eugene, Irene, and Laura Heptner
Glenwood, Mills County, Iowa, about November 1910
(Notice the pig on the front porch!)

OLIVIA ANNA MARIA *OLIVE* HEPTNER
Born: May 4, 1904; Died: December 21, 1907
Buried: St. Paul's United Christian Church, Dumfries, Iowa

IRENE HEPTNER AND OLIVE HEPTNER
(Spring 1907)
Glenwood, Mills County, Iowa

Eugene Heptner on Fanny in Iowa
(About 1910)

Frank and Laura lived in that house until they moved to Campbell County, Wyoming, in the spring of 1914 where they were one of the original homesteaders in the Little Iowa community north of Rozet. Campbell County was only three years old when they arrived. It was created in 1911 out of parts of Crook and Weston Counties. Frank came from Iowa by himself early in 1913 on an emigrant train to look for land suitable for farming. He brought with him two horses, Fanny and Rex; one mule, Jenny; one milk cow named Hardy; a plow; and other farming equipment. In September 1913, he filed an original application for a homestead with the land office in Sundance, Crook County, Wyoming, for 320 acres located in Section 31, Range 69, Township 51 about 9 miles northeast of Rozet and about 16 miles northwest of Moorcroft, Crook County, Wyoming. He received the final Certificate on February 18, 1919.

DEPARTMENT OF THE INTERIOR

UNITED STATES LAND OFFICE

Sundance, Wyoming.

Sept. 19, 1913.

NOTICE OF ALLOWANCE.

Frank H. Heptner

Rozet, Wyoming.

Sir:

Your homestead application , SERIAL No. 09575 ,

Receipt No. 1248482 , for E½ SE¼, sec. 30; E½ NW¼, N½ NE¼, sec. 31;

and N½ NW¼ , Section 32

Township 51 North, Range 69 West , 6th Principal Meridian,

has been this day allowed, subject to your further compliance with

law and regulations applicable thereto.

This not being a coal township, according to the records of this

office, your consent to the reservation of the coal to the U. S.

is unnecessary, and is hereby rejected.

Very respectfully,

_____ , Register.

_____ , Receiver.

NOTE.—The homestead law contemplates that residence shall be established immediately after entry, where not established before that time. Failure to establish residence within six months will forfeit the entry, if proven upon contest or final proof, unless it be shown that the entryman has been prevented, by climatic conditions, sickness, or other unavoidable cause, from establishing residence within six months immediately following entry; in such event his failure may be excused, provided it be shown that actual residence was not delayed beyond twelve months from the date of entry. An application for extension of time to begin residence will not ordinarily be considered except upon contest or final proof. Leave of absence can not be granted, for any cause, unless the entryman has established bona fide residence.

Laura Young Heptner was unable to accompany her husband to Wyoming because her mother, Frieda Young was ill, so she stayed in Iowa to help take care of her. Her mother died on May 13, 1914. After helping her brothers and sisters to bury their mother, Laura, at the age of 30, said good-bye to her family in Council Bluffs, Iowa. Then, with her four children, Irene age 8, Eugene age 6, Oscar age 4, and Leona age 2, by her side she boarded an emigrant train bound for Campbell County, Wyoming. They arrived at Moorcroft, Wyoming, on May 31, 1914 (Irene's eighth birthday) where Frank met them with a team of horses and a wagon. On the train with them came two horses, Old Tat and Queen, some furniture, trunks filled with the necessities to set up their new home, and other family memorabilia that would keep them in touch with family and friends that Laura and her children had left behind in Iowa.

Emigrant train similar to that which Frank & then Laura with their children rode from
Glenwood, Mills County, Iowa, to Moorcroft, Wyoming, in 1914

Team and wagon like the one Frank Heptner
met his family at Moorcroft to take his family
to the Heptner homestead about 16 miles northwest
of Moorcroft, Wyoming – 1914

After loading all their belongings in the wagon, the family began the last leg of their move west to Wyoming. The family stopped at the Thomas and Drucilla Johnson homestead on Well Creek for a welcome cool drink of water before continuing towards their new home. It has been said that when Laura Heptner looked north from the top of *The Divide* towards the site of her new home, she, in great dismay, wondered aloud, "What a god forsaken country this is!" As she scanned the landscape before her she saw wide vistas of sagebrush-covered hills and canyons with an occasional cottonwood tree and no other houses in sight except the small one room tarpapered house that her husband had quickly put up before his family arrived. She probably would have been more than happy to turn around and go back to Iowa, but there was barely enough money to get started on the homestead let alone to purchase a return train ticket back to Iowa. So, she and her children went forward with fear and determination to help her husband build a new life in this desolate land that was so different from where she had lived all her life in Mills County, Iowa.

About 1923

Laura soon discovered that there were kindly neighbors living among those hills and canyons. The Heptners arrived too late in that Wyoming spring to put in a garden or a crop. Their first winter in Wyoming was a hard one for the family. However, the neighbors shared their garden produce with the Heptner family. Eugene Heptner remembered the family coming home one evening to find a quarter of beef hanging on the side of the house. The family was afraid of eating the meat, but finally decided to try it. It became a welcomed piece of food for them. They never found out who gave the side of beef to them. Soon thereafter the family could purchase a few milk cows with calves. The family became dependent upon cream checks to pay for groceries for many years. Another source of cash was hogs. They were turned into the fields after the corn was harvested to fatten up, and then they were driven on foot to Rozet to be shipped on the train to Omaha and sold for slaughter.

The first thing Frank built in 1914 was a root cellar. This cellar was not only used for storing canned meat and vegetables, it was also used as a storm shelter. Laura would gather all her children and take them to this root cellar during summer storms. Having lived all her life in Iowa, she had a great fear of storms and tornadoes.

The communities the Heptners had moved to were locally named *Little Iowa* located towards the east, and *Cottonwood Valley* located northwest of the Heptner homestead. Within these communities there were many group gatherings held at each other's homesteads. At these box socials, dances, and carry-in dinners, the neighbors visited about crops and the weather, played music and cards. The children played games. From these activities, and others, they built a community who depended on each other in both the good times and the tough times.

38

The Heptner family lived north of The Divide; Charlie and Minnie Woods and their children: Viola, Gerald Jed, Bertha, Lillian, Clarence, Harold, and June, lived east of the Heptner homestead. Flora Ranney, her daughter Eunice and son Harley and her grandchildren, Blanche, Genevieve, and David Ernst, lived east of the Charley Woods place. George and Clara Jensen lived north of the Whisler homestead in Cottonwood Valley. Frank and Marna Kuehne lived north and west of the Heptner homestead. Carl and Esther Kuehne lived east of his brother Frank. Carl Kuehne died of a heart attack on February 7, 1925. Later Esther married his brother, Herman Kuehne. They moved to Big Springs, Nebraska, where the parents of Herman, Carl, and Frank lived. Other neighbors included George and Grace Spencer and their daughter Nora, who was the wife of Charlie Hinds; Will and Myrtle Spencer and their children, Esther and Emery, and two grandsons, Lester and Donald McCune (when they left for Minnesota, Henry Deafie and Daphne Edwards bought their place); Fred L. and Matilda Jane Hamm and their children Adolph, Winifred, Dorothy, Gladys, Alfred, Bessie, and Mildred, lived north and east of the Heptner homestead.

The immediate area in which Frank and Laura Heptner homesteaded was known as *Little Iowa* as other families, mostly from Iowa, moved into the community and filed for homesteads. They were all hard-working, kindly people and soon became good neighbors offering each other a helping hand when needed. There was no school for Irene and Eugene to attend that first fall 1914. A schoolhouse was being built about two miles east of the Heptner homestead. It was named the Cottonwood School (later in the 1930s it would be renamed the Woods School). The Cottonwood School opened in the fall of 1915 with Edna Stewart, who had just finished the eighth grade, as the school's first teacher. Irene and Eugene both entered the first grade that fall together. Irene had attended the first and second grades in Mills County, but with the family's move west they felt it would be better for her to repeat the grades. The children sat on nail kegs with planks of wood for desks until the school board was able to purchase or make desks.

New families continued to move into the area until there were about twelve living in the Little Iowa community. As the community came to life with the subsequent births of their children, they also experienced the inevitable family deaths. When Vern Woods, 17-year-old son of Oran and Mary Woods, died on October 10, 1817, from a broken neck when a corral pole fell on him during branding, Charles H. Simpson donated land for a cemetery. It was located across the road from the Fayette Thompson homestead along the Miller Creek road about fifteen miles northeast of Rozet near the Crook County line. After his burial, the men gathered in the Little Iowa schoolhouse across the road to discuss the cemetery. Each man there gave a donation to help build a fence and make improvements. They laid out the plots and then fenced it in and named it the Little Iowa Cemetery. In return, they were given plots in their names. Later, an unexpected deal was offered on the price of a cemetery gate. The company had a gate that had never been paid for and offered it at a much-reduced rate. Hence the cemetery was renamed Pleasant Valley Cemetery, as it is known today. Faye Thompson took care of the cemetery for many years. After him, his son and daughter-in-law, Wilbur *Bill*, and Lucille Thompson kept the burial record books, assigned plots, and dug the graves. Their daughter, Kay Thompson Shepherd, keeps the books today (2018).

The Heptner family grew with the birth of Wallace Edwin on January 29, 1918. He was remembered as a nice baby, always smiling, with bright blue eyes and curly hair. He lived only until two months past his first birthday. He died on Saturday, March 29, 1919, from Spanish influenza. While his mother prepared her baby son for burial, dressing him in his good clothes, his father made a burial box for him. He was buried in the Pleasant Valley Cemetery on Sunday, March 30, 1919, with a short service, attended by neighbors and officiated over by the Reverend H. A. Toland. The following poem was printed in the Rozet Items of the Campbell County Record, April 5, 1919:

"Goodbye little one till we meet again,
    In that blessed world of light.
Where there's no more sorrow, sickness or pain,
    Where never comes the night.

We'll miss you as we begin the day,
    We'll miss you at noonday as we gather around the board,
We'll miss you as the shadows chase the light away,
    But we'll never miss you in the presence of the Lord."

The family continued to grow with the births of Jeanette Louise on March 1, 1920, and Walter on August 8, 1922, who lived only one day. He was buried alongside his brother in the Little Iowa Cemetery.

About 1917 or 1918 a blizzard came which afterwards caused several of the families to pack up and leave, abandoning their homesteads. Some returned to Iowa, others moved to other locations in the west. In May 1922, another blizzard began with heavy rain before turning into snow. The storm lasted three days and many horses and cattle died. More discouraged people left the Little Iowa community, but the Heptners stayed.

Frank, Laura, and their children learned to cope with tough times. The Spanish flu epidemic of 1918 and 1919 devastated the community. Whole families were stricken. There was no help but a nurse who went from house to house. The Little Iowa Cemetery began to fill. Despite this they believed their misfortunes were mixed with blessings. There was plenty of coal and wood for the taking. Women gave birth at home with the help of a neighbor. Laura, herself, helped many neighbors through sicknesses and childbirths. They had rigged up a pioneer fence telephone system; which did not always work when a doctor was needed. Jeanette liked to say. "The doctor got there for me. I have a doctor-signed birth certificate." Leona recalls how her mother always dreaded leaving the children alone when their father had to take her to a neighbor who needed help. Their mother would take blankets and other necessary things to the storage cellar and leave a kerosene lantern for light. She was afraid to have the children keep a fire going for warmth, so the children bundled under heavy blankets as they played games until their father returned. Sometimes their mother would return in a day, other times she wouldn't return for several days. Throughout these tough times the neighborly spirit of the community always prevailed.

Despite their hardships, the Heptners endured by participating with their neighbors at barn dances, card parties, and other social gatherings in the people's homes and at the school house. The children presented school programs for their hardworking parents and neighbors. One Christmas Eugene sang Silent Night in German (*Stille Nacht*). The Heptner children played with the other children in the community. One summer tradition was seeing how many of the neighbor's watermelons they could eat the heart out of without getting caught. Irene, Eugene, and Oscar hilariously recalled many close calls in their later years. During one incident, when the owner of the watermelon patch interrupted the children, they dropped the knife they had with them as they ran out of the patch. Irene, because she was the fastest runner, was elected as the one to go back after it. The children also attended Sunday school held in the Cottonwood School. Their lessons were taught by the Rev. H. A. Toland, a Methodist minister who lived near his son John, and daughter Ona (a school teacher), who homesteaded about one-half mile southeast of Rozet.

Water was scarce; fresh running streams were not available. Soon after the Heptner family arrived, Frank made a hand-dug well in a creek east of the house. The well was not very deep. The water was good, and they enjoyed it. The neighbors enjoyed it, too. They would come with a team and wagon and a rain barrel or two to fill up with water from that well. Quite often there would be at least three or four teams and wagons lined up to get water. The first one in line would get his barrels filled. The next one in line had to wait until the well filled up with water before he could fill his rain barrel. This continued until everyone finished filling their rain barrels. The time spent waiting for water was very likely spent visiting with each other, commenting on the weather, the crops, their families, and any of the current topics that were of interest to them - an early version of today's *water-fountain* review board. After the land was officially surveyed it was found that the well was not on the Heptner property, but on the Woods homestead! Another hand-dug well was dug in the early 1930s. Eugene Heptner and Harley Ranney dug it. The well was a deep one, about nineteen feet deep. It was good water. At first, they dipped the water out with a pail tied to a rope long enough to reach the water. Later, they put a hand pump in the well and set up a windmill.

Jeanette recalls a story about a wandering gosling's adventure in the well. "One day someone left the opening to the well uncovered. Geese were walking to and fro around the well, and when Leona and I went to investigate we found a little gosling floating around on the water at the bottom of the well. We couldn't leave him down there. At first, we tried to get him in a pail that we lowered down to where he was. We could get him in the pail, but there was enough water in the pail that he was able to kick himself out before we could pull the pail out of the water. After Leona and I talked the situation over, I allowed Leona to tie a rope around me and lower me down into the well. There were bricks around the water line, so I had a place to stand. Then she lowered the pail down into the well. I caught the gosling and put it in the empty pail. Since there was no water in the pail he could not get himself out, and Leona pulled him up and out of the well safely. Then she pulled me up out of there."

Each member of the Heptner family shared each day's work on the homestead. They worked to clear the fields, plant crops, and establish a garden. Work began in the spring as soon as the soil could be worked and continued until the first snow arrived in the fall. The open range with no fences caused problems with the long-horned cattle that ranged freely. Frank assigned Irene the task of riding herd on the long-horned cattle that threatened their crops and garden. She got up every two hours during the night to chase the cattle out of the fields. This continued throughout the daytime also. One summer she was promised her own saddle when the crops were sold if she succeeded in keeping the cattle out of the fields. Irene never got her saddle because a hailstorm flattened the fields before the crops could be harvested. Rattlesnakes were always watched for. Frank killed at least thirty-five on one trip to Rozet. Rattlesnake hunts were common throughout the county because they were abundant everywhere at that time. Eugene and Oscar helped their father with branding cattle, cutting poles from cedar trees in the hills to build corrals for their milk cows. Soon a barn and corrals, a granary, and an icehouse were built. Hay was cut and stacked manually by Frank and his oldest children during the summer. In the fall, the butchering of a hog was a full day's task. The boys assisted in the butchering, the girls helped their mother clean the intestines that would be used as casings for the homemade sausage. The meat was ground up and fried and then stored in the rendered fat in large crock jars. Blood was saved to make blood pudding. Headcheese and cornmeal mush (sort of like scrapple) was made from the hog's head; the ears, feet, and tail were pickled. They planted potatoes and a garden that was tended by Laura and the girls. Produce from the garden was picked, dug, and then canned or stored in the root cellar for use in the winter months. During the winter blocks of ice were cut from the reservoir and stored in sawdust in the icehouse for summer use. Frank and the children fed hay to the cattle almost daily especially when the winter was a long and snowy one. One winter when it was exceptionally cold Irene suffered severe frostbite in her hands when driving the team of horses while her father pitched the hay off of the hayrack for the cattle. She spent Christmas day that year being hand fed her dinner. When not needed at home, the children attended school during the winter months.

The Heptner homestead was in School District Four. In the fall of 1924 when their oldest daughter, Irene, was ready to enter high school, they moved south over the divide to the Fischer place, which was in School District Three. From there the children rode a school bus/wagon to Rozet to attend the Rozet Consolidated School. One of their bus drivers was Slim Whisler. Eugene and Oscar also drove the bus some of the time. That September 1924 when Irene entered Rozet High School as a freshman, Eugene entered the eighth grade, Oscar and Leona entered the seventh grade. In September 1927, Jeanette joined them as she entered the first grade with Alma Day as her teacher. After the death of their father, Eugene and Oscar did not return to school. Irene graduated from Rozet High School in May 1928. Shortly afterwards, Laura took her family back to Glenwood, Mills County, Iowa, to visit her sisters and brothers and for her children to meet their many cousins. After returning from Iowa, Irene attended the Teacher's Institute that summer at

41

the University of Wyoming in Laramie. That fall Laura continued to live at the Fischer place, so Leona and Jeanette could continue to attend school at Rozet without paying tuition.Transportation in those early days was by horseback, wagon, or foot.

When Frank Heptner needed to travel to Gillette for business, he would walk the nine miles to Rozet to save his horses. He then would catch a freight train in Rozet and ride in the caboose to Gillette. After finishing his business, he would return by train in the caboose to Rozet and then walk home. On those occasions when he had to obtain supplies he would drive his team and wagon to Gillette which would take two to three days before he arrived back at home. Consequently, these trips were not taken unless they were absolutely necessary. He purchased his first car, a Chevrolet, in 1927. Jeanette remembers riding in it with her father and mother sometime in the summer of 1927. They were living at the Fischer place at the time and had been to a community carry-in at the Ranneys. She didn't remember the drive to Ranneys and believes that either Oscar or Eugene drove the car there. Apparently, Irene, Eugene, Oscar, and Leona had other ways to get home, so her father drove Jeanette and her Mother home in that Chevy. Jeanette sat between her mom and dad, sitting close to her mother so that her legs would not get in her father's way. He had to drive down a steep incline, cross a spring in the creek bottom, and then up a steep incline on the other side. Two 2x4 boards were laid across this spring. They were just wide enough for the car wheels to fit on. If the driver failed to keep the wheels square on these boards the car would fall off and into the creek and be quite stuck. This evening was a very frightening experience for Jeanette and her mother, as her father complained that there was something the matter with the car. He said the gearshift was not working properly and that the steering wheel was not turning as easily as it should. This caused them to worry about crossing the spring creek. Jeanette remembers the drive until they were safely across the spring, then she apparently fell asleep because she didn't remember getting home. The next day, Eugene and Oscar drove the car to check it out, but nothing was found wrong. Shortly after that Frank Heptner suffered a series of strokes and died on March 3, 1928. The family felt that he might have been suffering early symptoms that summer evening while driving his family home.

Jeanette recalls: "While we were living at the Fischer place the Heptner family quite often went to dances in a big red barn somewhere in the community. Ida Wells played the organ, and Paul Grunke played a violin. At first the evening was a lot of fun until I became tired. Then the organ's gasping for breath and the squeak, squeak of the violin got the best of me. I went to the lower part of the barn and found a nice bundle of hay to lie on. I know my intentions were to lie there until the family was ready to go home. It didn't work out that way. I fell asleep, and the family went home without me! For a long time after that I didn't like the sound of violin playing. However, at one of our teacher's conventions the program consisted of a violin player. He first explained the mountain lore of a certain mountain area and then he played a tune representing that area. I loved it. Now I have to say that I like violin music—sometimes."

In 1929 after Oscar's marriage to Dorothy Catherine Whisler on June 5th, they moved to the Fischer Place. His mother had moved back to the Heptner homestead with Irene, Eugene, Leona, and Jeanette. That fall Leona stayed with Oscar and Dorothy, so she could complete her senior year of high school at Rozet. Laura was determined to continue working the homestead with the assistance of her children. After teaching two years at the Deer Creek School, on July 2, 1930, Irene married Carroll Duvall *Slim* Whisler. They moved to the Whisler homestead about three miles west of the Heptner homestead along the Adon Road. Leona began her first teaching assignment at the Cottonwood Valley School along the Adon Road, northwest of the Heptner homestead. Oscar and Dorothy's first child, Darleen LaVonne was born on October 6, 1930. In or about 1931 Laura and Eugene bought their first tractor. Jeanette remembers its clog wheels. In the fall of 1931, Eugene entered Campbell County High School as a junior. But, because of demands at the homestead, he was unable to graduate. During the 1930s the drought was so bad the Heptners didn't have any grass and no hay. They had to sell their cows. The cattle were driven to Rozet, put on the train, and shipped to market. The cows seemed to know this was their last trip as they walked up the divide. They walked one behind the other, making a long single line of about twenty cows. These cows were sold to the government just to be slaughtered. No one got the use of the meat. This was during the era of President Franklin D. Roosevelt. It was his attempt to control the economy. Six milk cows were kept so they still had milk and cream. The Great Depression left many people in the community in debt. With no crops or cattle to sell they turned everything over to the Federal Land Bank and left. Again, the Heptners stayed. "We couldn't raise enough money to leave," recalled Eugene Heptner. Eugene hunted coyotes and rabbits for bounty money, worked for the WPA, and around at various places wherever he could find work. During the summer, after the birth of Darrell Lelan Heptner on May 22, 1933, Oscar Heptner and Slim Whisler went to work for the Civilian Conservation and Construction (CCC). They both returned home before winter. ArLou Leona Whisler was born September 27, 1933. Her sister, Pearl Margaret, was born November 11, 1934. Leona continued teaching in the rural schools of Campbell and Crook Counties. Jeanette attended school at the Woods School (formerly the Cottonwood School) until she graduated from the eighth grade on June 5, 1935. Shirley Joyce Heptner was born on August 4, 1935.

In 1935 Laura bought a small lot with a small house on it on the corner of U.S. Highway 59 and Fourth Street in Gillette, Wyoming. She and Jeanette, along with Ellen Whisler, moved to town that September so Jeanette and Ellen could enter the Campbell County High School as freshmen. Laura found work washing dishes at the Stockman's Cafe—Tom Demos was the manager—to supplement her income. Lorna Jean Whisler was born on March 7, 1936. The grasshoppers came in 1936. As Jeanette remembers, they came like a cloud and left like a cloud leaving devastated crops and grassland behind them. They chewed everything in their sight, including the curtains, but left the onions till last. One of Jeanette's most vivid memories of that summer was watching the onions fall over one by one. Eugene, along with Harley Ranney, drove to Washington and Oregon to work in the fruit orchards. They returned to Rozet in September 1936 when Eugene was called home because his nieces, ArLou and Pearl Whisler, daughters of Irene and Slim Whisler, passed away two weeks apart from influenza. In 1937, Oscar and Dorothy along with their three children, Darleen, Darrell, and Shirley, and Dorothy's two youngest sisters Pauline and Evelyn, moved to Idaho Falls, Idaho, to work in the potato and vegetable fields. The next spring, they moved on to Oregon to pick fruit in the orchards. They returned to Rozet in 1939, living in a little white house in Rozet for a brief time. Leona, by 1939, was teaching the primary grades (first, second, and third) in the Rozet Consolidated School. Jeanette graduated from Campbell County High School on May 19, 1939. That fall she enrolled in the Normal Training Class given at the high school.

Times did get better by the time 1940 arrived. In the spring of 1940, Oscar and Dorothy rented and moved on to the Miller place, about five miles northeast of Rozet. Eugene finished building his reservoir that fall. Leona and Jeanette helped their sister Irene cook for threshers that summer. Olive Carroll Whisler was born on December 16, 1940. In January 1941, Laura began working for Mrs. Mankin's mother, Mrs. Butler, and Eugene finished building Eunice Ranney's house in Gillette on the corner of U.S. 59 and Fifth Street. Eunice's brother, Harley, had passed away on October 27, 1940. Slim Whisler was helping Oscar build on his house at the Miller Place. Laura quit working for Mrs. Butler and went to work again at the Stockman's Café until she moved back to the Heptner homestead in March 1941. Jeanette started to work for Mrs. Butler on April 8, 1941. She quit on April 20, 1941 to take a job with Mrs. Baird who was ill and needed someone to care for her three children. However, Mrs. Baird quickly recovered and by April 23, Jeanette was out of a job. Eugene's new threshing machine arrived August 6, 1941. Jeanette accepted her first teaching position at the Upper Cabin Creek School in Crook County. However, with the bombing of Pearl Harbor by the Japanese on December 7, 1941, things changed once more. They learned how to cope with oil, gas, and sugar rationing during World War II. Leona and Jeanette were both teaching school. Eugene, Oscar, and Slim were kept busy with putting up hay, cutting, and threshing grain in the summer; hog butchering in the fall; cutting and storing ice, feeding cattle and sheep in the winter; planting crops, shearing sheep, calving and branding in the spring, threshing wheat and oats for themselves and then for their neighbors during the late summer and early fall. Threshing days were much like *barn-raising* days. All the neighbors came with their teams and wagons to help each other to thresh their crops and store the grain. Laura and her daughters planted and tended gardens. They were kept busy in the fall preserving and storing garden produce in the cellars along with preserving pork meat at butchering time. In the spring of 1944, Darleen, the oldest daughter of Oscar and Dorothy lost her eyesight from brain tumor surgery at the Mayo Clinic in Rochester, Minnesota. She was thirteen years old. During this decade Eugene and Leona filed on another 320 acres, and they were able to buy some of the abandoned land from the Federal Land Bank. If such land was kept for twenty years, the owner received all the mineral rights. Those who kept the land were rewarded when oil was discovered in the area in the 1960s, among them the Heptners.

Laura Heptner, age 66, died on October 10, 1950 at the Mayo Clinic in Rochester, Minnesota, after a lengthy illness. She left a large void in the lives of her surviving children, grandchildren, and her many friends and neighbors. Grandma Heptner, as she was known, not only by her grandchildren but also by others living in the long extinct *Little Iowa* community and the Rozet area would be remembered for her kindnesses and her ready assistance to help where needed throughout her life. She was buried alongside her husband, Frank, and her two baby sons in the Pleasant Valley Cemetery.

Laura Heptner and her children, taken on
New Year's Day 1950
At Oscar and Dorothy's on the Miller Place

Laura Margarete (Young) Heptner
1883 – 1950

The life of this homesteader's wife in northeastern Wyoming in the early 20th century was stark, lonesome, and harsh in the best of times. It became clear to her soon after her arrival in 1914 that the weather and other elements of nature would always be hostile towards her and her family. Summer produced heat, wind and lack of rain, severe thunderstorms, and hailstorms. Winter brought snow, below zero temperatures, and occasional, but always severe, blizzards. Grandma Heptner and her husband Frank accepted these insurmountable challenges to keep their little family under shelter and made the appropriate improvements required to receive full title to their homestead. Despite their efforts, Wyoming soil never became like the *rich black soil* that was abundant in Iowa. However, despite their original limitations, Grandma Heptner and her children continued to live on the farm after her husband and her children's father's death on March 3, 1928. Together they cleared the land of sagebrush and cactus to increase their pasture and to make new fields for grain and hay.

After her death, her oldest son, Eugene Heptner, continued to work and develop the homestead for the rest of his life. He and his brother, Oscar, who eventually owned a ranch south of the Heptner homestead along the now South Heptner Road, helped each other with the heavy work of maintaining their land and raising cattle and sheep. They grew alfalfa, wheat, oats, and rye from time to time. In the later years they just grew hay for their cattle and sheep.

Laura Heptner's Family - Three Generations

Irene (Heptner) Whisler, Leona, Oscar, Eugene, and Jeanette Heptner
about 1976

ArLou Whisler (1933-1936)
Pearl Whisler (1934-1936)

Darleen (Heptner) McGraw Heptner, Grandma Heptner, Olive Whisler,
Shirley (Heptner) Prazma, Lorna Whisler, Darrell Heptner
1941

Jerry McGraw, Mary Kay (Heptner-Isham) Jones, Randy Prazma,
DeeDe Heptner-Isham, Bruce McGraw, Marleen (Prazma) Cooper
Christmas 1959

Corina Sue (Heptner) Allen
1966

Merlyn McGraw, and
Kim (McGraw) Longtin   1965

46

THE HEPTNER HOMESTEAD
(About 1917/18)
Frank, Laura, their children, Irene, Eugene, Oscar, and Leona
with several children from the Little Iowa community (probably of the Woods and Hamm families)

Issued April 10, 1917, by the State of Wyoming,
Board of Livestock Commissioners

47

BRANDING CATTLE
(about 1917/1918)

Irene Heptner on Fanny keeping an eye on the cattle waiting to be branded;
the long-horned cow was *Hardy,* their main milk cow

Frank Heptner, on the left, George Spencer on the right holding the calf with a rope
while Charlie Hinds brands the calf.

Leona Heptner, age 5, on Fanny
(About 1917)

Leona, about age 8, with Rex
at the Sam Weaver Place
(About 1920)

Jenny, the mule

Fanny, Rex, and Jenny came to Wyoming in 1913 from Iowa with Frank on the emigrant train, along with a milk cow named *Hardy*, a plow, and some farm equipment.

Wallace Edwin Heptner
Born: January 29, 1918; Died: March 29, 1919

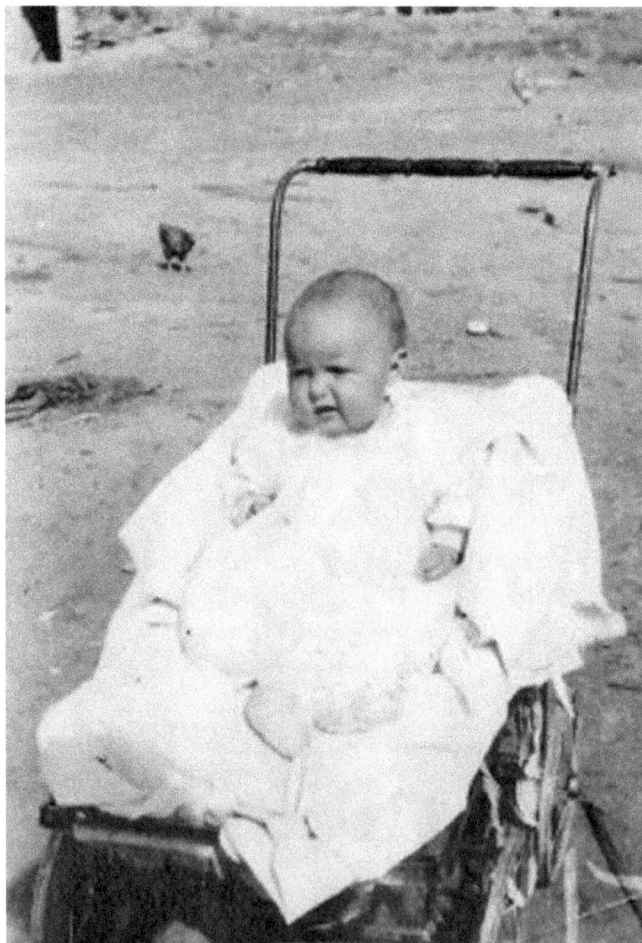

Jeanette Louise Heptner
Born: March 1, 1920
(The storm cellar in the background was the
first thing her father built when he arrived in 1913)

Laura Heptner, holding Jeanette,
with Leona and Oscar
(Fall 1920)

Jed Woods, Oscar Heptner, with their dog (name unknown),
and Eugene Heptner, about 1920

BEST BUDDIES!
Harold Woods, Jeanette Heptner, Virgil Jensen,
June Woods, and Frederick Jensen
(About 1922)

Note: The Woods children pictured above were children of Charley and Minnie Woods; the Jensen children were the children of George and Clara (Thompson) Jensen.

Frank Heptner and sons, Eugene and Oscar
hauling corral poles home after a day of cutting them down in the hills east of the homestead
about 1920

THRESHING WHEAT OR RYE

Threshing grain at the Charlie Woods place, located about a mile east of the Heptner homestead.
The horses are Old Tat and Queen who came from Iowa on the emigrant train.

A FEW *LITTLE IOWA* NEIGHBORS
(1923)

About 1924

Adults, l-r: George Jensen, Frank Kuehne, Frank Heptner, Charlie Woods, Eunice Ranney, Minnie
Woods, _____, Marna Kuehne, Harley Ranney, Laura Heptner, Esther Spencer
Kuehne, Carl Kuehne, Flora Ranney, and Clara Jensen, holding Virgil.

Children: Frederick Jensen, David Ernest, Genevieve Ernest, June Woods, Jeanette Heptner, and
Harold Woods

COOLING OFF ON A HOT SUMMER'S DAY – about 1926
(Esther Spencer, Lois Ernst, Blanche Ernst, Leona, and Irene Heptner,
on the bank is Jeanette Heptner)

Leona on the rake, Oscar and Eugene operating the
buck rake, and Frank on top of the stack – about 1925

STACKING STRAW FROM THE THRESHED GRAINS
(Summer 1927)

55

Frank and Laura Heptner Move their family to the Fischer Place
in School District Three
(1924)

Eugene Heptner is the tall boy in the back row, about 3rd person from the left
Irene Heptner is the back row about the 7th person left of Eugene.
Leona and Oscar are probably in the photo, but I could not find them. (ljw)

They moved because their homestead was in School District Four and, for Irene to attend high school at Rozet located in School District Three, they would have had to pay tuition. So they moved the family a few miles south to the Fischer place in School District Three. Oscar and his sister, Leona, entered the seventh grade at Rozet, Eugene entered the eighth grade, and Irene entered the ninth grade. They all rode the school bus/wagon to school. During the 1927-1928 term Slim Whisler was the school bus driver. The family returned to the homestead before 1930.

Irene and Leona Heptner at the Fischer Place
About 1924

THE FRANK AND LAURA HEPTNER FAMILY
Frank, Oscar, Eugene, Laura, Jeanette, Irene, Leona
taken at the Fischer place
about 1926
Frank Heptner died March 3, 1928

LAURA HEPTNER'S TRIP BACK TO MILLS COUNTY, IOWA
(Summer 1928)

Standing: Leona Heptner, Walter Huelle, Aunt Emma (Young) Boehm,
Laura (Young) Heptner, Aunt Lydia (Young) Basch,
Irene Heptner, Grace Basch

Front: Uncle Herman Basch, LaVonne Huelle, Jeanette Heptner

A 1927 Chevrolet Sedan
Similar to the first car Frank Heptner bought

THANKSGIVING DAY AT GRANDMA HEPTNER'S
(1933)

Eugene, Jeanette, Laura, Leona, Irene Whisler, Oscar

Back Row:	Jeanette Heptner, Laura Heptner, Eugene Heptner, Elmer Whisler, Leonard Whisler, Oscar Heptner (holding Darrell) Ton Whisler, Eunice Ranney, Slim Whisler
Middle:	Ellen Whisler, Ruth Whisler, Leona Heptner, Pauline Whisler, Blanche Ernst, Mildred Whisler, Dean Whisler
Front:	Phil Whisler, Eurith Whisler, Joan (Joann) Whisler, Darleen Heptner, Alberta Whisler, Allen Whisler, Harley Ranney

A HEPTNER/WHISLER GATHERING
at
Slim and Irene Whisler's home

(Probably Irene's birthday May 31, 1936)

Standing: Laura Heptner, holding Pearl Whisler, ArLou Whisler, Irene Whisler, Darleen Heptner, Marge Whisler and Pauline Whisler sitting on the water barrel

Sitting: Paul Reed, a neighbor, David Whisler holding Allen Whisler, Ton Whisler holding Alberta Whisler, Jeanette Heptner peeking over Ton's shoulder, Mildred Whisler holding Joan (Joann) Whisler, Ellen Whisler behind Dorothy Heptner who is holding Shirley Heptner, Slim Whisler, Dean Whisler in front on the ground, Oscar and Darrell Heptner on the ground, and Eugene Heptner lying on the cot.

(Note: Lorna Whisler, born March 7th, and Donnie Whisler, born May 25th, were asleep inside)

ArLou and Pearl Whisler, New Year's Day 1936
They died in September 1936 two weeks apart
from influenza

Thanksgiving Day, November 1936

Back Row: Eugene Heptner, Jeanette Heptner, Evelyn Whisler, Grandma Heptner,
Dorothy Heptner holding Shirley, Pauline Whisler, Irene Whisler holding
Lorna Whisler, Ellen Whisler, Slim Whisler
Front Row: Darrell Heptner, Dean Whisler, Darleen Heptner

GRANDMA HEPTNER and HER GRANDCHILDREN

Darrell Heptner, ArLou Whisler,
and Darleen Heptner – 1934

Darleen, Shirley, Lorna, and Darrell
Thanksgiving 1936

Shirley Heptner, Lorna Whisler, Darrell and
Darleen Heptner on Red
(1938)

GRANDMA HEPTNER WITH HER CHILDREN
AND HER GRANDCHILDREN
Jeanette, Leona, Oscar, Irene Whisler, Eugene,
Darleen Heptner, Shirley Heptner, Grandma Heptner holding
Olive Whisler, Lorna Whisler, and Darrell Heptner

Irene and Slim Whisler

Oscar and Dorothy Heptner

63

The Heptner Homestead in the 1940s

Before electricity

After electricity in the 1950s

THE LAURA HEPTNER FAMILY
at the home of Slim and Irene Whisler
(1947)
Back: Oscar Heptner, Laura Heptner, Slim Whisler, Irene Whisler,
        Jeanette Heptner, Darleen Heptner, Eugene Heptner (hidden),
        Dorothy Heptner, Leona Heptner
Front: Shirley Heptner, Lorna Whisler, Olive Whisler, Darrell Heptner

Laura Heptner and her children, taken on
New Year's Day 1950
At Oscar and Dorothy's on the Miller Place

1925

1975

THE HEPTNER BROTHERS AND SISTERS
Irene, Eugene, Oscar, Leona, and Jeanette

The Heptner Family - December 2001
Standing: Olive Whisler, Darrell Heptner, Robert Prazma, Shirley Prazma, Lorna Whisler
Sitting: Audrey Heptner, Aunt Jeanette Heptner, Darleen Heptner

IRENE LYDIA HEPTNER
and
CARROLL DUVALL *Slim* WHISLER

Carroll Duvall *Slim* Whisler

Irene Lydia (Heptner) Whisler

About 1980 - the year they celebrated their 50th wedding anniversary

    Irene Lydia Heptner arrived in Rozet, Wyoming, on May 31, 1914, her eighth birthday. She came with her mother and two brothers and one sister on an emigrant train from Glenwood, Mills County, Iowa. Her father met them at the train station in Moorcroft, Wyoming, with a wagon and a team of horses to take them to their new home north of Rozet what became known as the *Little Iowa* community. Having completed the first and second grades in Glenwood, Iowa, Irene was looking forward to attending school that fall. However, upon the family's arrival at the Heptner homestead they learned there would be no school available that fall for the children to attend.   A schoolhouse was being built on the Charlie Woods home-stead and it wouldn't be ready until September 1915. Although Irene had begun school in Iowa, her parents decided she should repeat the grades because of her not being able to attend school in Wyoming for a year. So, Irene and her brother, Eugene, re-entered the first grade at the Cottonwoods School in September 1915. Her teacher was Edna Stewart, who had just completed the eighth grade that May. Irene attended the Cottonwood School through the eighth grade. However, because she was needed at home many times to help her mother, she was not able to graduate from the eighth grade until May 1924.

The Cottonwoods School - 1918
Eugene 1st in back row; Irene last in back row
Leona 1st in front row; Oscar last in front row

Because the homestead was in School District Four, her father and mother moved the family south about two miles, over the divide, to the Fischer place. It was in School District Three. This move allowed Irene to enter Rozet High School as a freshman in September 1924 and Eugene, Oscar, and Leona to attend classes in the Rozet Consolidated School without their parents paying tuition. Irene, Eugene, and Oscar played high school basketball. In September 1927 when Irene entered her senior year, Jeanette entered the first grade at Rozet with Alma Day as her teacher. Their father died on March 3, 1928, after a series of strokes.

Rozet High School, Rozet, Wyoming

Senior Class – fall 1927
Mary Brennan, Russ Moon, Mary Gardner,
Hamilton Davis, Irene Heptner

Junior Class – fall 1927
Faye Johnson, Gilbert Moran, George Moon,
Doris Riley

Sophomore Class – fall 1927
Dick Brennan, Joe Slattery, Ione Riley,
Leona Heptner, Dorothy Whisler,
Laine Gardner, Thelma Hoxsie, Eugene
Heptner, Eileen Brennan, Oscar Heptner

Freshman Class – fall 1927
Lester Hoxsie, Cleo Cook, Marvel Riley,
David Whisler

Irene graduated from Rozet High School in May 1928.

That summer of 1928 Irene enrolled in summer school in the Teacher's Institute at the University of Wyoming, Laramie, Wyoming. In September, she accepted a teaching position at the Deer Creek School, north of the Whisler homestead alongside the Adon Road. She taught there for two years. Her students were Virgil Jensen and Alvina Weaver.

Three Generations
Carroll Duvall Whisler, age about six months,
Pearl Vida (Duvall) Whisler
Catherine (Slade) Duvall Clark

Carroll Duvall *Slim* Whisler was born October 2, 1905, in Tecumseh, Johnson County, Nebraska, to David Riley and Pearl Vida (Duvall) Whisler. He was the eldest child of sixteen children born to Riley and Vida. Only nine of Slim's brothers and sisters lived to adulthood. He grew up in Tecumseh and Pawnee County. By the age of twelve he was helping his father in the fields and sawing wood for the family during the winter. He started school in Mayberry, Pawnee County, Nebraska. He completed his first through seventh grades there. In 1919 Riley and Vida, Slim, now age thirteen, and five brothers and sisters, moved to Hartstrong, Yuma County, Colorado located about seventeen miles southwest of Eckley, Colorado. There he continued to help his father farm. Because he was able to attend school only two to three months in the year, he never received his eighth-grade diploma. In the summer, he worked in the harvest fields and in the winter, he shucked corn for neighbors. Soon, however, it became apparent that the dry conditions of the area made their attempts at farming unsuccessful. Riley Whisler began thinking about looking for another place to live. In 1922 after hearing about the Rozet area from James Duvall, his brother-in-law, Riley Whisler with his oldest sons, Carroll, Elmer, and Ton drove north out of Colorado, through Nebraska, to Campbell County, Wyoming. The truck was loaded with household furniture, chickens, and other equipment. Vida and the remaining children came later with the assistance of her brother, James Duvall. (*See Appendix A for A Brief History of the Whisler Family*)

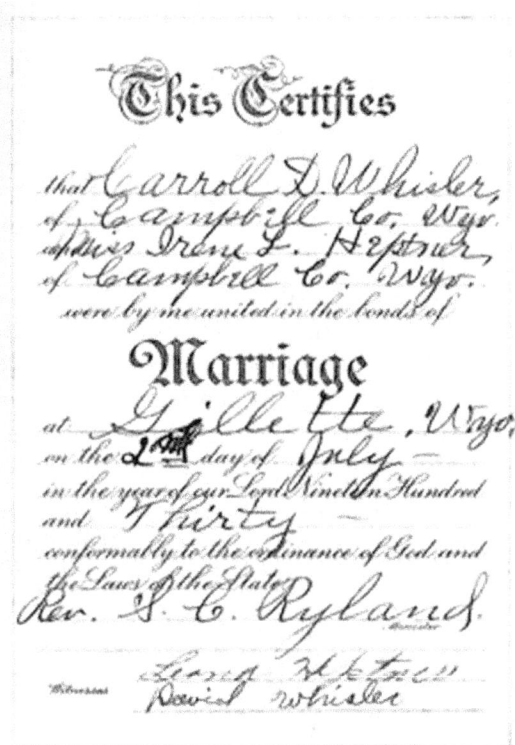

July 2, 1930
Gillette, Wyoming

Slim and Irene – December 25, 1930
Rozet, Wyoming

Slim and Irene Heptner were married on June 2, 1930, in the Presbyterian Church's manse, Gillette, Wyoming, officiated by the Rev. Samuel Ryland, with Leona Heptner and David Whisler as witnesses.

After their marriage, Irene and Slim Whisler made room on the Whisler homestead for Slim's younger brothers, Leonard, age 12, and Dean, age 6. They attended school at the Deer Creek School. When Leonard was ready for high school, he lived with Dorothy and Oscar Heptner and sometimes with his brother, Ton and Mildred Whisler. Leonard graduated from Rozet High School in 1939. When Dean was ready for high school he lived with Ton and Mildred Whisler during the school months; he did not graduate. Instead, he enlisted in the U. S. Navy after the attack on Pearl Harbor on December 7, 1941. Leonard enlisted in the U. S. Army and was assigned to the Army's Calvary Division at Fort Lewis, Washington. However, shortly afterwards the Calvary Divisions of the Army were disbanded, and Leonard was given a medical discharge due to him having flat feet.

Starting a life together on the edge of the coming Great Depression took courage, determination and a lot of fortitude. Irene and Slim continued to prove up on his father's homestead. He planted wheat and oats and raised a few head of cattle. Irene kept track of the cattle (she had lots of earlier experience) while Slim tended to the fields. They grew a garden, planting potatoes, beans (both dry and green), corn, peas, and whatever else they could get to grow. One year they grew gigantic pumpkins. Irene canned many quarts of pumpkin for pies that year. The 1930s brought them hardship and tragedy. During the Great Depression Slim hunted coyotes for the bounty paid by the County Commissioners. He also trapped rabbits and other small animals such as skunk and badgers for their pelts which he sold to Sears and Roebuck to help feed the family. Irene and Slim became the parents of four daughters. Their first daughter, ArLou Leona, was born September 27, 1933. By 1934 it was so dry that the crops did not amount to anything that summer. Slim went to work for the Civilian Conservation and Construction Corps (CCC) building roads between Moorcroft and the Devil's Tower. He came home for the birth of their second daughter, Pearl Margaret, November 11, 1934. Slim began driving Dean to school at Rozet in September 1935. In November, he put stucco on the house. The next year he built a wind charger to charge batteries, so they could have electric lights in the house. Lorna Jean, their third daughter, was born March 7, 1936. August and September of 1936 Slim worked on the schoolhouse at Rozet. That fall, Irene and Slim lost their two oldest daughters from influenza. Pearl Margaret died September 18th and ArLou Leona died September 30th, 1936. They were both buried in the Rozet Cemetery, one mile south of the Rozet School. As Slim stated in his diary extracts for 1937: "Hauled Dean to school in Rozet. I worked on cars and trucks in winter. We were still hauling drinking water; had to borrow money from the Rural Resettlement Program to operate farm on. School warrants for transporting Dean to school and grants from relief help us to get by. I worked on county bridges and roads when they washed out; cut wheat and oats for neighbors when we could. Grasshoppers were bad." One summer they hauled water for their cattle because the reservoirs went dry. Slim also helped his brother-in-law, Eugene Heptner, thresh grain for the neighbors; they built a telephone line between them and the Heptner's. In the fall of 1938 he returned to Anselmo, Nebraska, to work for Robert Poor shucking corn. In the late 1930s Slim began working for the Smith Implement Company during the winter months. In 1939, he helped Eugene build Eunice and Harley Ranney's house on the corner of U. S. 59 and Fifth Street in Gillette, Wyoming. Harley Ranney never moved into the house as he passed away October 27, 1940. Harley was buried in the Pleasant Valley Cemetery beside his mother Flora. On December 16, 1940, their fourth daughter, Olive Carroll was born.

World War II came and brought additional hardships with the rationing of oil, gas, and sugar. Slim's youngest brother, Dean, enlisted in the Navy in December 1942, at the age of 18. In September 1942 Lorna was ready for the first grade. There were not enough students living around the Whisler homestead to warrant placing a country school in the area. So Slim drove her to school at the Rozet Consolidated School during her first year in school. Her teacher at Rozet was Miss Leona Heptner! The next school year starting in September 1943, there were enough students to set up a school. David and Marge Whisler were then living on the Woods place across the road from Grandma Heptner. Their two oldest children, Donnie and Delores, and Lorna added up to the required three students needed for a school to be set up. A schoolhouse was moved about half way between the Whisler and Heptner homesteads. The school was named the Whisler School. Their teacher, for the next three school terms, was Miss Jeanette Heptner! In September 1944 Donnie and Delores' younger sister Barbara joined them. Olive joined them for a few days of the month for an early kindergarten in 1945.

Slim had no time for but a few pastimes, one was playing soft/baseball. In the 1920s he played on the Rozet team from time to time, when he had the time. Because of his long hits he was nicknamed *Babe*. His other love was flying. In 1945, he took flying lessons. After receiving his license, he enjoyed flying out to look for cattle for Irene who was on horseback. When he dipped his wings, she knew where they were and would go gather them up and bring them to the corral. During the winter of 1949 when Slim was working in Gillette, Irene and the girls were snowed in for over a month. As soon as the blizzard ended he flew over the house and dropped the mail and the *Denver Post* to them. He also flew over the Heptner ranch and dropped cartons of cigarettes for Eugene. He was a member of the Wyoming Flying Farmers.

When Lorna was ready for high school in September 1950, Slim rented a small house in Gillette for the family to live in so she could begin her freshman year in Campbell County High School. Olive entered the fifth grade in the Gillette Grade School. Then he bought one half of Grandma Heptner's lot on Fourth Street in Gillette and moved a small house on to it during the summer of 1951. In 1968, they bought a house at 105 West Valley Drive, across the railroad tracks and north of Gillette Main Street. They lived there for the rest of their lives.

After moving to town Slim tried to continue farming on the homestead but soon he had to give it up. For several summers to supplement his income Slim baled hay for ranches from Gillette to Upton and Sundance, Wyoming. In chokecherry season, he always took time to pick a pail or two and bring home for Irene to make jelly for hot biscuits and syrup for pancakes. Eventually, he sold the ranch in June 1971 to Raymond *Red* and Phyllis (Johnson) Record. In 1960 Slim quit working at the Smith Implement Garage and went to work for the County Commissioners maintaining roads and bridges in the summer and plowing snow in the winter. He worked from six to six most days and a lot of weekends. About 1971 he quit the county and went to work for Paul's Truck and Tractor building oilrig location sites. He retired in the middle 1976.

Irene took in ironing to provide her with some spending money. She also became involved with the United Presbyterian Women at the First Presbyterian Church. Later she joined the Rebekah Lodge and the Retired Teachers Association. Her favorite pastime was crocheting doilies, tablecloths, etc., and embroidering pillow cases and dish towels as gifts for her nieces and nephews and friends. She also made up a large number of these items for the Presbyterian Church's Annual Fall Bazaar.

In their retirement years, Irene and Slim's health declined. They did manage to make several trips to Virginia to spend some time with their daughters, Lorna and Olive. Slim passed away on June 7, 1983, from heart disease; Irene passed away on November 9, 1983, from complications of cancer and several strokes. They are both buried in Pleasant Valley Cemetery near their parents.

The Whisler Homestead

About 1980
No one has lived here since about 1951. From the left one can see the equipment shed where Slim parked his tractors, farm equipment, and his Taylorcraft airplane; two granaries, the well; the grove of trees is gone except two or three; the bunkhouse and the original two-room house; Slim's garage, and lastly the upper and lower barns. Slim and Irene sold their place in the 1970s to Raymond *Red* and Phyllis (Johnson) Record. They built a house and barns across the creek to the northwest.

Irene Heptner - 1928
University of Wyoming

Slim Whisler – 1928

Dean, age 7, Irene, and Slim at Devil's Tower
1931

Whisler Homestead - 1936

The year Slim built a wind charger to charge batteries
so they could have electric lights in the house.

Slim and Irene – 1932

Dean Whisler, age 10 – 1934

Slim and Irene and ArLou Whisler
1934

Slim Whisler
(With a badger pelt)
1934

Eighty-one rabbit and badger pelts that Slim hunted
(shot thru the head) and dried to be
sold to Sears Roebuck
1934

Slim and his Fordson Tractor – 1934

Slim smoothing out the ruts on the Adon Road - 1935

Slim hauling corral poles – 1935

BINDING WHEAT FOR THRESHING
1935
Slim Whisler on the binder and Eugene Heptner on the tractor

THE YEAR OF THE BIG PUMPKINS!
Slim, Leonard, and Dean Whisler
1935

Slim, Leonard, and Dean picking and husking corn – 1935

CIVIL CONSERVATION CONSTRUCTION (CCC)
1935

Constructing the curve,
Slim Whisler on right with
his slip and team of horses

Constructing a road between Moorcroft and Devil's Tower

The bend in the road completed

Lunch break; Ton Whisler on right

ArLou Leona and Irene
Spring 1934

Grandma Heptner, Jeanette, Irene holding Pearl, and
Slim with ArLou – August 1935

ArLou and Pearl on New Year's Day 1936
Pearl died, age 1½: September 18, 1936
ArLou died, age 3:   September 28, 1936

Dean, Irene, Lorna, Slim
Spring 1937

Slim and his favorite vehicles!

Slim Whisler and his red convertible – 1925

Family lore tells us that it was burned up with the help of his two sisters, Ellen and Pauline. They were
stacking hay; the girls were bored, so Slim put them to work cleaning up around the hay stack.
Deciding it was taking too long the sisters decided to enlist the help of a little fire to
make their job go faster. Understandably, their brother was not happy with their decision.

Slim's Model A Truck - 1936

Dean Whisler with Lorna - 1937

Slim with Lorna - spring 1937

Leonard Whisler and Lorna
Fall 1938

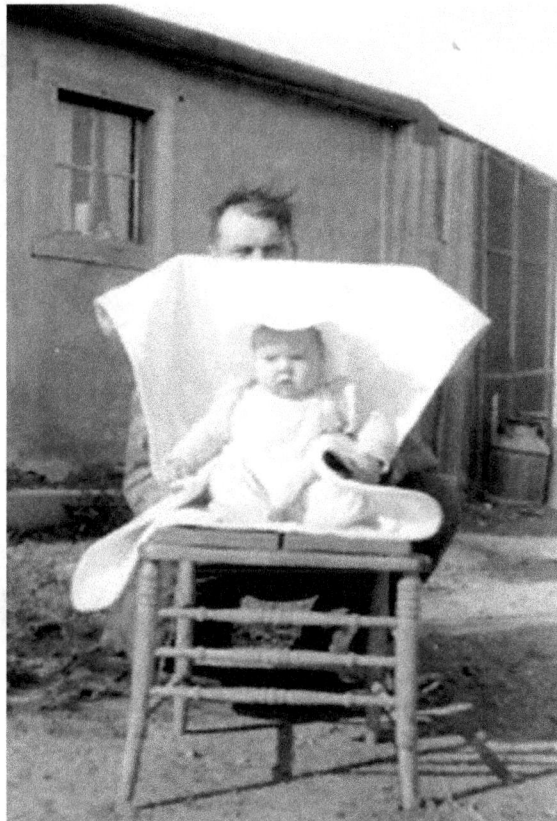

Olive Carroll and Slim peeking
over the chair to see if Irene is ready to take
the picture – Spring 1941

Slim, Irene, Lorna, and Olive at the Rozet Cemetery
May 1941

Olive and Lorna
Dec 1941

Grandma Heptner and Olive
Spring 1941

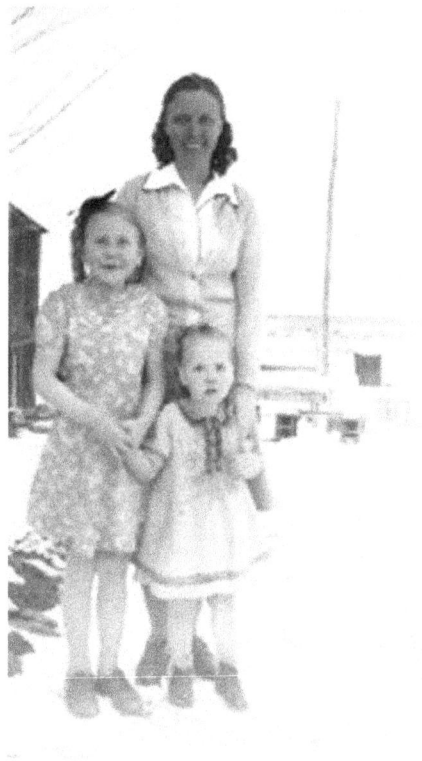

Leona Heptner with Lorna and Olive
March 7, 1943

Slim, Irene, Lorna, and Olive Whisler
late Fall 1942
(Photo taken at Eunice Ranney's
house at Fifth Street and U. S.
Highway 59, Gillette, Wyoming)

Slim, Irene, Dean, Olive, and Lorna
(Summer 1944)

Slim Whisler and his Taylorcraft Airplane
1945

Slim was a member of the Wyoming Flying Farmers

Slim Whisler watching his brother, Elmer,
repair his binder
1948

Slim Whisler and Olive with his new combine and old tractor
About 1945

Winter of 1949 – January into February

New Year's Day – Jan 1, 1949
Donnie Whisler, ____, ____, Ferris Cook,
Leonard Whisler, Melvin Donner, Ed Wolff,
Slim Whisler sitting on sled; kids unknown
They had been jack-rabbit hunting

Dad's Garage after being shoveled out

Chicken House and lower barn and corrals

Road after being plowed out

Slim putting chains on the car

Dean and Helen Whisler came visiting
by team and sled

Irene carrying water for washing dishes

Slim getting ready to take off to go back to Gillette to work
January 1949

Slim Whisler with his new combine
1949

Irene helping Slim cut wood- summer mid-1950s

Olive and Lorna on their first day of school
in Gillette Grade School and Campbell County High School
September 1949
In front of the house in Gillette that
Slim rented when Lorna began high school

Slim bought half of Grandma Heptner's lot on 4th Street in Gillette east of the Douglas Highway and moved a small four-room house upon a poured cement block basement that leaked like a sieve every time there was a heavy melting of winter snow or summer rains. There was a kitchen, dining room, living room, and a bedroom on the first floor—no closets, no bathroom. In the basement, there were three storage rooms and Lorna and Olive's bedroom. They learned to keep everything off the floor in the spring and to pull their clothes in bed with them to warm up in the winter. Irene and Slim lived there from 1951 until they bought another house on the north side of town in the early 1970s.

Olive's graduation from Hastings College, Hastings, Nebraska
May 27, 1962

Hastings College Chapel
Hastings College (Presbyterian), Hastings, Nebraska
1962

Slim and his hay baling outfit about 10 miles east of Upton, Wyoming
August 1964

Irene and Slim picking chokecherries on the ranch
ten miles east from Upton, Wyoming, where he was baling hay
August 1964

Slim's road grader he operated to level off oil field sites
For Paul's Truck and Tractor Service
March 1965

THE SLIM AND IRENE WHISLER FARM
(1964)

THE SLIM AND IRENE WHISLER FAMILY

Irene, Slim, Lorna, and Olive about 1948

Slim, Lorna, Irene, Olive
Taken in Arlington, Virginia, in 1968

ArLou Leona (1933-1936)   Pearl Margaret 1934-1936)   Lorna Jean Class of 1954   Olive Carroll Class of 1958

Campbell County High School

ArLou Leona was born September 27, 1933, and **Pearl Margaret** was born November 11, 1934. They died in September 1936 from the influenza; Pearl on the 18th and ArLou on the 30th. They were buried in the Rozet Cemetery just below their cousins, Joann, Alberta and Charles Whisler children of Ton and Mildred Whisler.

Lorna Jean, was born March 7, 1936. She attended the first grade at Rozet Consolidated School; her teacher was Leona Heptner. For grades 2-7 she attended the Whisler School where her teachers were Jeanette Heptner, Eurith Whisler, Bonnie Nielson, and Selma Raudsep. No teacher was found to teach at the Whisler School; Lorna completed the 8th grade at the Rozet Consolidated School; Dorothy Greer Addison was her teacher. The family moved to Gillette in 1949 when she began high school that September. After graduating from Campbell County High School in May 1954, she went to work for the Mountain States Telegraph and Telephone Company as a telephone operator. The chief operator/supervisor was Mrs. Josephine Lucas. Lorna worked there for about four and a half years until the telephone company was converting into a dial system which would no longer require operators at the Gillette office. In December 1959, she passed a federal civil service test and was classified as a clerk-typist, (GS-203-2). She was assigned to the Bureau of Naval Personnel in Arlington, Virginia, across the Potomac River from Washington, D. C. She began work on February 16, 1959, as clerk-typist in the Distribution Division responsible for distribution of Navy officers and enlisted personnel to and from their duty assignments throughout their careers. In 1980, as the Head of the Travel Order Section, (GS-209-09), Lorna was assigned to the automation of Navy travel nominations/orders (AUTONOM) Task Force. For her contributions toward the automation of Navy personnel travel orders, she was presented with the Navy's Superior Civilian Service Award on December 26, 1982. She retired on November 3, 1995, as Assistant head of the Travel Orders Section, (GS-209-12), in the Distribution Department of the Navy Military Personnel Command (formerly the Bureau of Naval Personnel) and is now living in Natural Bridge, Virginia.

Olive Carroll was born December 16, 1940. She attended grades 1-3 at the Whisler School; grade 4 at Rozet; and grades 5-8 at the Gillette Elementary School; graduated from the Campbell County High School in May 1958. That fall she entered Hastings College (Presbyterian) in Hastings, Nebraska, as a freshman. She graduated in June 1962 with a Bachelor's Degree in English. That fall she returned to Hastings to complete a major in Geography. She was encouraged to apply for a teaching-assistantship at the University of Maryland, which would help pay expenses and give her some experience in the classroom. She filled out the application and went home for Christmas and New Year holidays. When she returned to Hastings she learned she was accepted and that she had to be in College Park, Maryland, by the end of January. She packed up and moved to Arlington, Virginia, where she stayed with her sister Lorna after the spring semester. Olive graduated from the University of Maryland with a Master's Degree in Geography in August 1965. She went to work with the Defense Intelligence Agency, Arlington, Virginia, and later transferred to the National Library of Medicine, located on the grounds of the National Institutes of Health, in Bethesda, Maryland. Olive retired from the Library in June 1995 and now lives in Daleville, Virginia.

EUGENE JOHANN ANTON HEPTNER

Eugene Heptner was six years old when he came to Wyoming in May 1914 with his parents, Frank and Laura Heptner. They homesteaded about nine miles north of Rozet. Although he was ready for school that first fall, there was no school available until 1915. A schoolhouse was being built about two miles east of the homestead. It was named the Cottonwood School. In September 1915, Eugene and his sister Irene walked to school and entered the first grade together. Oscar joined them in September 1916 and Leona in 1918. In 1924 when Irene was ready for high school, his parents moved the family to the Fischer place, about two miles south, over the divide, so they could send their children to school at Rozet without paying tuition. Eugene entered high school at Rozet the fall of 1926. He played basketball with his brother, Oscar, Dan Brennan, Hamilton Davis, Tom Garrett, Russell Moon, George Moon, and Gilbert Moran. The Rozet basketball team was participating in the Northeast High School Basketball Tournament when his father died March 3, 1928. Neither Eugene nor Oscar returned to school after their father's death. They stayed home to help their mother run the homestead. In 1929 his brother Oscar married Dorothy Whisler and they moved to the Fischer place after Eugene, Irene, Leona, Jeanette, and their mother had moved back to the homestead. Leona did stay with Oscar and Dorothy from September 1929 until May 1930 when she graduated from Rozet High School.

In September 1931, Eugene returned to school, entering the Campbell County High School as a junior. However, he never graduated because he was needed at home and was unable to attend the required number of days to graduate. About 1931 Eugene bought a tractor to help work the fields. Jeanette remembers only that it had clog wheels. Farming was difficult during the 1930s as the weather was dry and nothing grew enough to be harvested. For extra cash money during these depression years Eugene hunted coyotes and rabbits for their bounty, worked for farmers or ranchers near or further away when work could be found, and he also worked for the WPA. In September 1935 his mother and sister Jeanette, along with Ellen Whisler, moved to Gillette so Jeanette and Ellen could attend high school. Eugene lived on the homestead alone. In the summer of 1936, Eugene and Harley Ranney drove to Washington and Oregon to look for work in the fruit orchards. Eugene was called home when his nieces, ArLou and Pearl Whisler, died in late September from the influenza. In 1938 his brother, Oscar, and family moved to Idaho and Oregon to work in the vegetable fields or fruit orchards. They returned to Rozet in the spring of 1939. His mother worked at the Stockman's Cafe while Jeanette and Ellen attend high school.

By 1940, things were looking up a little. Oscar and his family were now living on the Miller place, about four miles northeast of Rozet. Eugene and Oscar helped each other and their mother with planting crops, working cattle, and sheep on both the Heptner homestead and on the Miller place. Their brother-in-law, Slim Whisler, also helped when he could with stacking hay, cutting and threshing grain, putting up ice in the winter time, and other chores that needed an extra hand from time to time. Eugene began building a reservoir north of the homestead in summer of 1940, and he finished it that November. Always handy with carpentry work, Eugene started building a house for Eunice Ranney and her brother Harley in 1939. The house was not finished until 1941 because Harley became ill and then passed away on October 27, 1940. Eugene's mother moved back to the homestead in March 1941. On August 6, 1941, a new threshing machine arrived at the homestead. Eugene could not only thresh their wheat and oats, but also threshed for neighbors who did not have a threshing machine. Jeanette began her first year of teaching at the Upper Cabin Creek School in Crook County. Eugene and his mother drove her to the Charles Holbin place where Jeanette would board while teaching school that term.

Then with the bombing of Pearl Harbor by the Japanese on December 7, 1941, life again changed for the Heptners and their neighbors. They learned how to cope with rationing of oil, gas, and sugar among other things. Eugene and Oscar continued to plant wheat and oats; they put in new hay fields and worked their cattle and sheep. They shipped their cattle to Omaha for sale to the feedlots there. They would drive the cattle to the stockyards at Rozet, load the cattle onto cattle cars on the railroad, and then ride in the caboose to Omaha to supervise the sale of the cattle. In 1946 Eugene and Slim Whisler took their nephew, Darrell Heptner, with them. He was thirteen years old. Darrell returned with a new candy bar to show everyone—a Baby Ruth!!

Eugene continued to live on the Heptner homestead after the death of his mother, Laura Heptner, on October 10, 1950. He began to only raise sheep and cattle. He converted his wheat and oats fields into alfalfa hay fields. Later he quit raising sheep and kept only cattle. He and his brother now owned neighboring ranches. Oscar and Dorothy moved in 1952 from the Miller place east of Rozet into a newly built home just north of the George place on Well Creek Road, later renamed the South Heptner Road. They worked together to build up both ranches with the help of Darrell Heptner, Eugene's only nephew, and a few of Dorothy's nephews who spent their summers with their Uncle Oscar and Aunt Dorothy. Leona and Jeanette, when not attending required summer school, also lived out on the ranch between school terms. They cooked meals for their brothers, the hired hands, and volunteer workers, planted large gardens, canned its fruits and vegetables for winter use, and washed and ironed everyone's clothes. They also helped their brothers in the hay fields when needed and did chores such as milking cows, separating the cream from the milk, and raising chickens for butchering and gathering eggs.

Eugene never married; however, he became a favorite uncle to his nieces and nephew. He always had time to make them Fox and Geese game boards; whittle wooden puzzle balls; teach them how to play cribbage; take them for rides out into his hay fields to see his *night time livestock* (deer) feeding off his hay fields; boat rides on his reservoir [the Jiggs Reservoir); and fishing for bullheads at the same reservoir. In 1962, he and his only nephew, Darrell Heptner, drove to Bremerton, Washington, to visit with Darrell's daughters, Mary Kay and DeeDe. While there they took in the World's Fair in Seattle, Washington. Eugene would hire high school boys; Ronnie Joslyn, son of Pete and LaVonne Joslyn, was one; and other men to help him on the ranch. One of these hired hands who stayed the longest was John Wiltrout followed by Barnie F. Headley. Barnie worked for Eugene until his death on May 6, 1973. Barnie was buried in Mt. Pisgah Cemetery, Gillette, Wyoming, on May 9, 1973. He was helping Eugene to build a reservoir, and the tractor he was driving rolled over on him. For many years in the fall Eugene also enjoyed guiding hunters for deer and antelope. Some of these hunters were his cousins from Iowa and others who came from several eastern states. He made many lifelong friendships among these eastern hunters.

Eugene joined the First Presbyterian Church in Gillette on January 12, 1947. He was a life-long member of the Farm Bureau and a board member of the Rozet Community Church which he and his brother, Oscar, were instrumental in restoring in 1965.

Fishing was another favorite pastime that Eugene enjoyed. He especially liked to go fishing in the summer at Meadowlark Lake, located on top of the Big Horn Mountains. Leona and Jeanette would go with him. He would get their lines ready, and then he would work on his. In a brief time after throwing their lines out into the water, Leona and Jeanette would each pull out a fish. Of course, Eugene took the fish off the lines. He would just finish when one of them would pull out another fish. He would take that fish off the hook and he would hear someone say, "I got a fish!" This would happen repeatedly. This made Eugene unhappy, because he couldn't get his own line out in the water to do some fishing. But he was happy that Leona and Jeanette caught enough fish for their evening meal, which they shared with everyone who went camping with them. Bob, Ruth, Paula, and Sherry Stanley went camping with them often, as did Lefty Husted and his family and the Bauman family. Eunice Ranney, their old friend and neighbor from their homestead days, often went with them until she was no longer comfortable sleeping in a camping tent. She passed away on September 6, 1973 and was buried beside her mother Flora and her brother Harley in the Pleasant Valley Cemetery, northeast of Rozet.

In his later years, when it became apparent that he shouldn't be staying at the ranch by himself during the winter months, he moved into Gillette with his sisters Leona and Jeanette. At that time, they were both retired and living at 412 Circle Drive. At first, he only stayed during the winter; eventually he stayed year-round. During those times, he enjoyed visiting with his old friends. Former hunters would drop in to see him on their trips through Wyoming. He would play cards with his sisters and old friends, especially Blanche (Ernst) Beck and her husband Bill, until they both passed away. Blanche's aunt, Eunice Ranney, was also a frequent card player along with Chris and Marie Larsen. He also made many new friends, especially his photographer friend, Allan Sicks. His brother Oscar passed away May 5, 1977. Eugene died one year and eight months later on January 6, 1979. The brothers are both buried in the Pleasant Valley Cemetery, northeast of Rozet.

The Heptner Ranch
North Heptner Road, Rozet, Campbell County, Wyoming
About 1974

Rozet High School Basketball Team 1927
Standing: Dan Brennan, Gilbert Moran, Coach _____, Oscar Heptner
Sitting: Russ Moon, Hamilton Davis, Eugene Heptner

Sophomore Class – 1928
Rozet High School
_____, Joe Slattery, Ione Riley. Leona Heptner, Dorothy Whisler, Laine Gardner,
_____, Eugene Heptner, _____, Oscar Heptner

ALBERT KNAPP   ELSIE BARNES

WILLIAM HARDIN

DOROTHY WILMOT   OLUF GREGERSEN

MERCEDES WHITE   ROSS HUGHES

EMMY WATSON

RUSSELL SOUTH   LILLIAN FAHLER

BUD SUTHERLAND   AVIS HACKETT

EUGENE HEPTNER

MACIL BROWN   OWEN HENDRICKS

Junior Class, Campbell County High School – 1932 Annual

EUGENE HEPTNER AND HARLEY RANNEY BEFORE THEY LEFT
FOR WASHINGTON TO PICK FRUIT
1936

Eugene Heptner and Harley Ranney

They pulled Harley's trailer house to Washington

Eugene stopped to visit with Oscar and Dorothy in Oregon

Elmer Whisler, Harley, and Ruth Whisler,
Phil and Eurith in Washington

Eugene Heptner and Elmer Whisler
picking fruit in Washington

Eugene Heptner working calves
in his corrals at the Heptner Ranch
(Sometime during the 1950s)

Eugene Heptner feeding *cake* to
his flock of sheep
(1950s)

JIGG'S (EUGENE HEPTNER) NEW RESERVOIR
July 5, 1959
Bob Hamm (back to camera), Eugene Heptner, Leona
Heptner and John Wiltrout - Photograph taken by
Eunice Ranney

DEER AND ANTELOPE HUNTING SEASON

Eugene Heptner, Bill Young, and Art Reinert
Cousins from Council Bluffs, Iowa (about 1954)

Eugene Heptner and Gerald Young (son of Bill Young)

Jeanette, Leona, and Eugene
at Meadowlark Lake in Big Horn Mountains

Picnic up Shell Canyon in the Big Horn Mountains
With the Cummings Family of Basin, Wyoming
Doug Cummings, Jeanette Heptner, Eugene Heptner, Jeff Cummings, Mrs. Myrtle Cummings,
Leona Heptner, Lee Cummings, and Ellen Cummings

Jeanette Heptner, Lorna Whisler, Leona Heptner
Taken late summer 1960 in Leona and Jeanette's sweet corn patch

LET'S PLAY CRIBBAGE!!!
August 1959
Eugene Heptner, Leona Heptner, John Wiltrout,
Slim Whisler, and Eunice Ranney

John Wiltrout, Eugene, Ronnie Joslyn
June 1962

John Wiltrout and Eugene rabbit hunting
About 1964

Dedication of the refurbished Rozet Community Church
1965
Rev. Ray Cornwall, Daphne Edwards, Oscar Heptner, Eugene Heptner, Evelyn Hamm,
Rev Gerald Case, Pastor at First Presbyterian Church, Gillette, Wyoming

Slim Whisler helping Eugene to cut hay
1975

Eugene making hay bales
1975

OSCAR HERMAN HEPTNER
and
DOROTHY CATHERINE WHISLER

Oscar Herman Heptner was almost four years old when he arrived in Rozet, Campbell County, Wyoming, on May 31, 1914. He came with his mother, his brother Eugene, and two sisters, Irene and Leona Heptner. Oscar attended the Cottonwood school from the fall of 1916 until spring of 1924. That fall his older sister Irene was ready for high school so his parents moved the family over the divide to the Fischer place. They moved because their homestead was in School District Four and for Irene to go to school at Rozet his parents would have had to pay tuition. So, they moved the family a few miles south into School District Three. Oscar and his sister Leona entered the seventh grade at Rozet, Eugene entered the eighth grade, and Irene entered the ninth grade. They all rode the school bus/wagon to school. Oscar, Eugene, and Irene played basketball after school hours. Quite often they would need a ride home. Jeanette remembers, "Mom would hitch up the team and wagon and drive to Rozet to get them. She would not let me sit on the wagon seat with her. She made me get down on the floor of the wagon so that should I fall asleep I wouldn't fall far. On one of those trips I was not the only one to fall asleep. Mom fell asleep too. When she woke up the horses had turned the wagon around and headed back home! So, her brothers and sister had to wait for a bit longer before they were picked up." After Oscar's father, Frank Heptner, died on March 3, 1928, Oscar and his brother quit school to assist their mother with the homestead.

On June 5, 1929, Oscar married Dorothy Catherine Whisler in the manse of the First Presbyterian Church, Gillette, Wyoming, with the Rev. Samuel Ryland officiating. Dorothy was born November 28, 1910 in Tecumseh, Johnson County, Nebraska, the first daughter born to David Riley and Pearl Vida (Duvall) Whisler. The family later moved to Mayberry, Pawnee County, Nebraska, where Dorothy began school with her brothers. Her mother and father moved again about 1919 to Eckley, Yuma County, Colorado. She attended school there with her brothers until 1923 when once again her father moved his family, this time to Rozet, Campbell County, Wyoming. Riley Whisler's brother-in-law, James Duvall, helped him move his family from Colorado to Wyoming. They first lived with Riley Whisler's mother-in-law, Catherine (Slade) Duvall Clark, until he rented the Frank George place on Well Creek road now known as the South Heptner Road. (*See Appendix A for a brief history of the Whisler family.*)

Oscar and Dorothy Heptner moved to the Fischer place shortly after they were married in 1929. Laura Heptner, Irene, Eugene, and Jeanette had moved back to the Heptner homestead two miles north of the Fischer place. Leona stayed with Oscar and Dorothy that following year, so she could finish her senior year at Rozet High School. One of Dorothy's younger sisters, Pauline Whisler, age 7, came to live with them. Later in 1934 her sister Ellen came to live after living a year with their Uncle Jim Duvall and a year with their grandmother Catherine (Slade) Duvall Clark, *Grandma Clark*. At that time their youngest sister, Evelyn, age 3, remained with Grandma Clark. In 1936 after the death of Grandma Clark, Evelyn also came to live with Oscar and Dorothy.

Oscar and Dorothy were the parents of three children. On October 4, 1930, their first child, Darleen LaVonne, was born at home on the Fischer place. In 1931 Oscar and Dorothy moved to the Harley Ranney place east of the Heptner homestead. By the time Darrell Lelan arrived on May 22, 1933, they had moved to a small house about a half-mile north of the Heptner homestead. In December 1933, Jeanette remembers, "Oscar and Dorothy were sitting in their car parked on Main Street in Gillette discussing what they could do for Darleen and Darrell for Christmas. During their conversation, Oscar noticed something green fluttering over by the fence. He got out to investigate it and found a twenty-dollar bill. Their kids got a little red wagon for Christmas!" During that summer Oscar and his brother-in-law, Slim Whisler, went to work for the Civilian Conservation Corps (CCC) building roads between Moorcroft and the Devils Tower and Sundance. That fall, Oscar was called home when Pauline became very ill with appendicitis. In May 1935 Ellen Whisler and Jeanette Heptner graduated from the Eighth Grade at the Woods School (formerly the Cottonwood School). Later that summer, on August 4, 1935, Oscar and Dorothy's youngest child, Shirley Joyce, was born. In 1936 the family moved to the Heptner homestead and lived with his mother, brother, and two younger sisters.

At the suggestion of Oscar's aunt and uncle, Aunt Lou (Young) and Uncle Bill Meppin, in 1937 they packed up their family, including Pauline and Evelyn Whisler, and moved to Idaho Falls, Idaho, to work in the potato fields. Ellen Whisler remained behind with Grandma Heptner (Laura) as she was attending Campbell County High School in Gillette. Dorothy's brother Elmer, and his family soon moved close by in Idaho Falls, and they all worked in the vegetable and potato fields. In 1938, Oscar moved the family again, this time to West Stayton, Oregon, where they found work picking apples and other fruit in the orchards there. In the spring of 1939 they returned to the Heptner homestead. Shortly after arriving home, Shirley, age four, was badly burned. She and her cousin, Alberta Whisler, were playing with matches and accidentally set her clothes on fire. That fall Oscar rented a small white house at Rozet where Darleen entered the fourth grade and Darrell the first grade at the Rozet Consolidated School. Darrell's teacher was, who else, Miss Leona Heptner. Oscar's sister, Jeanette, and Dorothy's sister, Ellen, graduated from Campbell County High School, Gillette, Wyoming, on May 19, 1939.

In the spring of 1940 Oscar and Dorothy rented the Boyd Miller place about four miles northeast of Rozet. Oscar made improvements on the house during the summer of 1941 with the assistance of his brother Eugene and Slim Whisler. That summer, on July 23, 1941, Allen and Alberta Whisler, Dorothy's nephew and niece, were tragically drowned in a reservoir near the home of their parents, Ton and Mildred Whisler. World War II was declared on December 7, 1941, after Japan bombed Pearl Harbor. Oscar and Dorothy, like their neighbors, began learning how to manage feeding their family with rationing of various items, such as sugar, oil, and gas. In December 1942, Dorothy's youngest brother, Dean Whisler, enlisted in the United States Navy. He was eighteen years old. The family suffered another tragedy, when in the spring of 1944, Dorothy and Oscar's daughter Darleen, age 13, lost her eyesight when she was operated on for a brain tumor at the Mayo Clinic in Rochester, Minnesota. Dorothy's youngest brother, Dean, came home on leave for sixty days in July 1944. His brothers and sisters had not seen him since they sent him off at the bus station in front of the Goings Hotel in Gillette in August 1942. When it was time for him to return, he had a tough time leaving and wished that they had not authorized so many days leave. That fall Dorothy and Oscar entered Darleen in the Colorado School for the Blind and Deaf, at Colorado Springs, Colorado. Dean Whisler was discharged from the Navy on January 3, 1946. He married Helen May Kottraba, daughter of Ray and Kathryn Kottraba, on September 14, 1946, in Lincoln, Nebraska. Evelyn Whisler, age 20, was married in Oscar and Dorothy's home on December 25, 1946, to Melvin Harvey Donner, son of Charlie and Dora Donner. Darleen Heptner graduated from high school at the Colorado School for the Blind and Deaf on June 5, 1950, in Colorado Springs, Colorado. That fall she began college at Northeastern Wyoming Community College, Sheridan, Wyoming. Oscar's mother, Laura Heptner, passed away on October 10, 1950. Darrell Heptner transferred from Rozet High School to Moorcroft High School in fall of 1950 as a junior. He graduated from the Moorcroft High School on May 14, 1952, and enlisted in the United States Navy on May 26, 1952. Shirley Heptner graduated from the Rozet High School on May 20, 1953.

Oscar and Dorothy remained on the Miller place until 1952. They bought the former Frank George place and Oscar built a new house for them to move into. As stated earlier in this book, Dorothy's father, Riley Whisler, had rented the Frank George place when he first moved to Rozet 1923 as a place to live for his large family. Oscar built up his ranch with the help of his son and his brother. He was handy with welding, and he designed and built iron stars, complete with lights, to be turned on during the Christmas holidays. He was an infamous teaser and loved to pull practical jokes on his nieces and nephews, and then, as they came along, on his grandchildren. He liked to hunt and for many years served as a guide along with his brother, Eugene, for eastern hunters. Some were his cousins from Iowa who came out to hunt the Rozet plains and hills for deer and antelope. Oscar passed away on May 5, 1977, in Newcastle, Wyoming, after a long bout with cancer. Dorothy continued to live there until health concerns caused her to move into the Parkview Senior Apartments, 301 West Warlow Drive, in Gillette, Wyoming, at the age of 88. Dorothy died July 2, 2001, in Gillette, Campbell County, Wyoming, and was buried alongside of her husband, Oscar, in Pleasant Valley Cemetery, Rozet, Wyoming.

Mr Oscar H. Heptner
and
Miss Dorothy C. Whisler
Announce their marriage
Wednesday June the fifth
One Thousand Nine Hundred
Twenty Nine
at
Gillette, Wyoming

Oscar and Dorothy (Whisler) Heptner
June 5, 1929

Oscar, Dorothy, and Darleen
at the Ranney Place
About 1932

Dorothy Heptner with Darrell and Darleen,
and their little red wagon at their home
north of the Heptner homestead
1934

118

1934 C.C.C.

Oscar Heptner on the caterpillar

The Wessex underpass

CCC Camp Site east of Rozet and north of railroad tracks

Oscar in the Chow Line 4th from right

Dorothy Heptner and her three younger sisters,
Pauline, Evelyn, and Ellen Whisler
Rozet, Wyoming, about 1935

Oscar, Dorothy, Darleen, Darrell, and Shirley
1936

Oscar, Dorothy, Darleen, Darrell, and Shirley
1937 when they left for Idaho

IDAHO FALLS, IDAHO
Summer 1937 - Summer 1938

Phil Whisler, Darleen Heptner, Evelyn Whisler
Darrell Heptner, and Eurith Whisler
Christmas 1937

Shirley Heptner, Darleen Heptner, Evelyn Whisler,
Darrell Heptner – Easter 1938

Darrell on the hay rack, with Darleen alongside of the road.
Idaho Falls, Idaho
1937

Dorothy, Oscar, Darleen
Shirley, Darrell – 1938

Evelyn Whisler, Darleen, Shirley,
and Darrell picking apples

Shirley, Darrell, and Darleen Heptner and Evelyn Whisler
1938

About 1939
Oscar, Darleen, Dorothy, Darrell, and Shirley Heptner after they returned to Wyoming from Oregon.
They lived in a white house in Rozet, Campbell County, Wyoming, prior to moving to the Miller Place

1939 at Rozet
Back row: Evelyn Whisler, Oscar Heptner, Dorothy (Whisler) Heptner,
Ton Whisler, Mildred (Day) Whisler holding Nancy (almost 1), Leonard Whisler, and Ellen Whisler
Front Row: Alberta Whisler, Shirley Heptner, Darrell Heptner, Allan Whisler, Sally Whisler, and Darleen Heptner

Darrell, Shirley, and Darleen
at the Miller Place - 1940

Shirley and Darrell with their dogs
at the Miller Place, Rozet, Wyoming
1941

Shirley, Darleen, Darrell Heptner
Miller Place, Rozet, Wyoming
1943

Leonard Whisler, Darleen, Darrell,
and Shirley Heptner and Lorna Whisler
1940

Darrell and Darleen Heptner, Evelyn Whisler,
and Shirley Heptner at the Miller Place
about 1945

Oscar with his new foal and its mother
Miller Place - 1945

Laura Heptner, Darleen Heptner, Evelyn Whisler,
Dorothy Heptner, at Darleen's graduation from High School at the
Colorado School for the Blind and Deaf, Colorado Springs, Colorado
June 5, 1950

Darleen's guests at her graduation: Back Row: Kitty and Betty Ruth Whisler,
Jeanette Heptner, Dorothy Heptner, Shirley Heptner, Laura Heptner, Eugene Heptner,
Leonard Whisler; in front Dorothy Ellen Whisler, Judy Whisler, Oscar Heptner
(taken in front of the dormitory that had recently burned down.)

The Oscar Heptner's New Home - 1952

The photo above shows the new home being constructed by Oscar Heptner of Rozet. This is the first of a complete new set of farm buildings the Heptner's will build. Your TCEA maintenance crew, working from Moorcroft and Gillette, completed construction of a power line extension to the site in March. The meter pole is just out of the photo to the right. Beyond the meter pole will be the site for the new barn. Electric power tools will be used during the completion of the interior of the house. The picturesque windmill will soon be replaced by an electrically operated automatic pressure water system.
(Page Four, *The Tri-County Kilowatt,* Sundance, Wyoming, April 1952)

THE OSCAR AND DOROTHY HEPTNER RANCH
1984
South Heptner Road
Rozet, Campbell County, Wyoming

127

Oscar, Darrell, Dorothy, Shirley, Darleen
About 1948

Dorothy Catherine (Whisler) Heptner
1988
Grandma Heptner, the 2nd

Darleen, Shirley, and Darrell Heptner
Christmas 1935

Darrell, Darleen, and Shirley Heptner
about 1942

Darrell, Darleen, and Shirley
Whisler Family Reunion – 2002

Darleen Lavonne Heptner

Darleen Lavonne Heptner was born on October 6, 1930. She attended the Woods School and then Rozet Consolidated School until she had surgery for a brain tumor at the Mayo Clinic, Rochester, Minnesota, which left her blind. Her parents enrolled her in the Colorado School for the Deaf and Blind in Colorado Springs, Colorado, where she graduated on June 5, 1950. That fall she attended the Sheridan Community College, Sheridan, Wyoming. Darleen married Gerald Marvin McGraw on June 5, 1951, in the First Presbyterian Church, Gillette, Wyoming. They moved to Cheyenne, Wyoming, where Gerald worked.   In 1953, she received a leader dog named Skipper from the Mile-High Kennel Club of Denver, Colorado. Darleen and Gerald became the parents of four children: Gerald Marvin, Jr., *Jerry*; Bruce Lelan; Merlyn Keith; amd Kimmberlee Catherine *Kim*.

Gerald Marvin, Jr. *Jerry* McGraw married:

1st, Carlotta *Bunny* Pisciotti on February 17, 1972, at the Corpus Christi Catholic Church, Newcastle, Wyoming; one daughter Dixie Jo was born. This marriage ended in divorce. Bunny died August 11, 1984, in Weston County, Wyoming.

2nd, Debbie Lynn Divis, on August 4, 1973, in Gillette, Campbell County, Wyoming; two sons, Jeremy Thomas and David Jon were born. This marriage also ended in divorce.

3rd, Shirley Didona Booth in July 1979, in Oscoda, Iosco County, Michigan; two sons, Joshua Michael and Kyle Aaron were born. Both Jerry and Shirley served in the U. S. Air Force. This marriage also ended in divorce.

4th, Julia Ann Jahnke in July 2005, in Las Vegas, Clark County, Nevada. After retiring from the U. S. Air Force, they moved to Rapid City, South Dakota. Jerry and Julia are the parents of one daughter, Jordynn Arianna. They currently live in Box Elder, South Dakota, near Rapid City.

Bruce Lelan McGraw married:

1st, Agnes Elizabeth Foster on March 29, 1980, at Las Vegas, Clark County, Nevada. Two children, Eric Dean and Sarah Beth, were born. This marriage ended in divorce.

2nd Diane Fischer in 1996. Bruce and Diane are the parents of one daughter, Ashley Lynne. This marriage ended in divorce.

Bruce currently lives in Palm Springs, California, with his partner, John McLeod.

Merlyn Keith McGraw married Janet Marie Rowley on April 9, 1983 in Las Vegas, Clark County, Nevada. They are the parents of three daughters: Jennifer Joyce, Tabatha Dawn Marie, and Michelle Lynn. Merlyn and Jan currently live in Elko, Nevada.

Kimmberlee Catherine *Kim* is the mother of four children: Nicholas Shawn *Nick* McGraw, Christine Lynn Ross, Jason Raymond Ross, and Catherine Marie *Katie* Ross. Kim currently lives with her husband, Joseph Duane Longtin, in Zimmerman, Minnesota. Her mother raised her oldest son *Nick* until he graduated from Wright High School, Wright, Campbell County, Wyoming.

Darleen and Gerald's marriage ended in divorce. On December 17, 1976, in Portland, Oregon, Darleen married Don Bolland. This marriage ended in divorce. She has spent most of her life working with and for the National Blind Association to improve the quality of life for blind and deaf individuals. After living many years in Cheyenne, Wyoming, and four years in Wright, Wyoming, she moved to Gillette, Wyoming. On August 17, 1985, she married William J. Orester, in Gillette. This marriage also ended in divorce. In her remaining years in Gillette she lived at the Parkview Senior Apartments, 301 West Warlow Drive, until 2010 when she moved to Elko, Nevada, to live with her son, Merlyn McGraw and his wife Jan. She died on November 14, 2013, in Elko, Nevada; her ashes were buried in Pleasant Valley Cemetery, Rozet, Wyoming, alongside her parents in May 2014.

Colorado School for the
Deaf and Blind, Colorado Springs, CO
1950

Gerald McGraw and Darleen Heptner
Wedding Day, June 2, 1951

Jerry, Bruce, Merlyn, and Kim McGraw
1965

Darrell Lelan Heptner

Darrell Lelan Heptner was born May 22, 1933. He attended the Rozet Consolidated and High School until his junior year when he transferred to Moorcroft High School for his senior year. He graduated from high school in 1951 and immediately joined the U. S. Navy. He was trained as a personnelman and served on board the USS Essex (CV-9). He was deployed to Hawaii, Okinawa, Japan, Philippines, China, Thailand, and Korea. He was transferred to the USS Hornet (CV-8) for three months prior to his discharge from the Navy on May 22, 1956, in Bremerton, Washington. Darrell and Barbara Joy Edmison were married on April 3, 1956, in Bremerton, Washington. They are the parents of two children: Mary Katherine *Mary Kay* and Karrie Dee *DeeDe*. Darrell and Joy moved to Rozet, Wyoming, in the fall of 1958. Darrell began working for Winland Dairy. This marriage ended in divorce in 1962, and Joy returned to Bremerton, Washington, with the girls. On November 1963 Darrell married Charlotte Darlene Ford. This marriage also ended in divorce.

On June 10, 1966, he married Audrey Jean (Robing) Ridenour in the First Presbyterian Church, Gillette, Wyoming. Audrey's first husband, Gerald Allen *Jerry* Ridenour, son of Leo and Gladys Ridenour, died from a farm machine accident in the spring of 1963. In 1966 Darrell went to work at the Black Hills Power and Light at Wyodak, Wyoming, until 1979 when he resigned to work full time ranching. Not only did he work to expand his own herd of cattle, he helped his mother and his Uncle Eugene with the haying, calving, and branding, etc. In 1967 Darrell adopted Audrey's daughter, Corina Sue Ridenour. Darrell and Audrey spent their annual summer vacations driving to Bremerton, Washington, to visit with his girls, Mary Kay and DeeDe. In the fall of 1967 Audrey began driving a school bus for the Rozet Grade School until she retired on June 2, 2002. She died November 16, 2008, at home and was buried in Pleasant Valley Cemetery, Rozet, Wyoming. Darrell continued living in his and Audrey's home until he died on August 1, 2014. He was buried alongside of Audrey in the Pleasant Valley Cemetery.

Mary Katherine graduated from high school in Bremerton, Washington. Shortly afterwards she moved to Rozet to live with her dad. Mary Kay married John Leslie Jones on June 18, 1983 at the First Presbyterian Church in Moorcroft, Wyoming. They have one son, John Henry, *Hank*. Mary Kay and John live at Rozet where they bought the old Rozet Post Office. Mary Kay works as a dental assistant in Gillette.

Karrie Dee *DeeDe* went to nursing school after graduating from high school in Bremerton, Washington, and later in 1989 she also moved to Gillette to live. DeeDe lived in Gillette for several years. She became a certified Emergency Medical Technical and moved to Hartford County, Connecticut, to work with an EMT Unit. Her EMT Unit responded to the Twin Towers attack on September 11, 2001, in New York City. DeeDe died November 2, 2015, in Manchester, Hartford County, Connecticut.

Corina Sue graduated from Campbell County High School in 1980. She married Neil Henry Allen on April 17, 1994, at Prince of Peace Lutheran Church, Gillette, Wyoming. He worked for Stockman's Motor Company, and Corina worked in the Parts Department of Stockman's Motor Company. This marriage ended in divorce in 2013. Corina currently lives in Gillette, Wyoming.

U. S Navy
Personnelman 3rd Class
USS ESSEX (CV-9)

Darrell and Audrey's Wedding Day
June 10, 1966

Darrell and Audrey Heptner Family
Audrey, Mary Kay., Darrell,
DeeDe and Corina
1976

Shirley Joyce Heptner

Shirley Joyce Heptner was born August 4, 1935. She attended grades 1-12 at Rozet Consolidated and High School; graduating from Rozet High School in 1953. On December 27, 1955, she married Robert Earl Prazma, the son of James and Anna (Sabatka) Prazma, in the First Presbyterian Church, Gillette, Wyoming. They are parents of two children: Randy Darrell and Marleen Joyce. Shirley worked for the Campbell County School District from 1971 until she retired in 1998. Robert worked for Pete's (Joslyn) Body Shop before going to work for Davis Chevrolet Garage in their body shop. Robert retired in 1993. Robert kept himself busy with helping his grandsons with their jobs—mowing lawns. He also kept an eye on his mother, Anna Prazma, who lived alone on the Prazma ranch east of Rozet until she moved into a Senior Citizens apartment in Moorcroft, Wyoming. Anna passed away on May 3, 2002, one month shy of the age of 95. Robert also kept an eye on his mother-in-law, Dorothy Heptner, also living alone on the Heptner ranch northeast of Rozet until she also moved into an apartment for senior citizens in Gillette. He also checked up on Shirley's aunts, Leona and Jeanette Heptner. Shirley and Robert lived in Gillette all their married lives. They enjoyed attending their grandsons' baseball and basketball games; making yearly trips to California—in their motorhome, to visit their son, Randy, who lived in Imperial Beach, California. Robert passed away on November 11, 2004, in Gillette, Wyoming, and is buried in Mt. Pisgah Cemetery, Gillette, Wyoming. Shirley currently lives in the Primrose Retirement Community, Gillette, Wyoming.

Randy Darrell Prazma attended grades 1-8 at the Gillette Elementary School and graduated from Campbell County High School in May 1972. He enlisted in the United States Navy and served in the submarine service. He was stationed in Okinawa, arriving there on January 19, 1975. He met a young lady also serving in the U. S. Navy. Randy and Mary Agnes Macfarlane were married on June 15, 1976, in Naha, Okinawa, Japan. They became parents of three children: James Oscar *Jimmy*, Randy Darrell, Jr., and Brooke Elizabeth. His marriage ended in divorce. Mary resigned from the Navy and moved with the children to Plattsburg, New York, to live. Randy resigned from the Navy and moved to Imperial Beach, California. Randy married Tamera Tami McDaniel. He operated a cab company in and around Imperial Beach, California, for many years. In 2016 he and his wife moved to West Colombia, South Carolina, where they currently reside.

Marleen Joyce Prazma attended grades 1-8 at the Gillette Elementary School and graduated from Campbell County High School on May 25, 1975. She married Donald Dale Cooper on April 24, 1976, in the First Baptist Church, in Gillette, Wyoming. They became the parents of two sons: Dustin Dale and Derek Donald. Both Dustin and Derek graduated from Campbell County High School and from the University of Wyoming, the alma mater of their great aunts, Leona and Jeanette. Marleen began working for the Campbell County School District in 1984, and Don has worked in mining for forty-one years. They have lived all their married lives in Gillette.

Graduation from Rozet High School
1953

Wedding Day
December 27, 1955

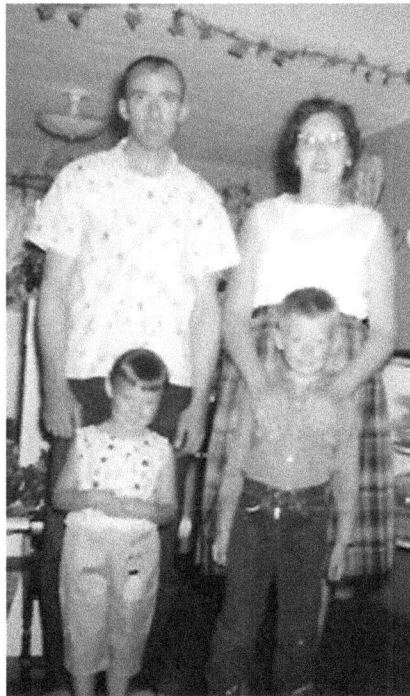

Shirley, Robert, Randy, and Marleen
About 1961

LEONA SOPHIA HEPTNER

Leona Sophia Heptner was one year and nine months old when she arrived in Campbell County, Wyoming, on May 31, 1914, with her parents Frank and Laura Heptner and her older sister, Irene, and brothers, Eugene, and Oscar. Also on board that train were their horses Rex and Fanny. She celebrated her second birthday on August 2, 1914. During the next few years she grew, watched, listened, and played with her sister and brothers and the neighboring children. As she observed them leaving to walk to school, she would wonder and wonder when she could go to school with them. Finally, in the fall of 1918 she proudly walked to school with them. She was in the first grade and beginning a lifelong love affair with school. The Cottonwood School was located about two miles east of the Heptner homestead. Her first-grade teacher was Edith George. Leona was so happy when she began learning how to read because "now she could read her own book." Her second-grade teacher was Mark Richmond. There were thirteen children attending the Cottonwood School that school term. The largest enrollment at the Cottonwood School was twenty-one students. Leona attended the Cottonwood School through the sixth grade.

In the fall of 1924 her older sister, Irene, was ready to begin high school. The nearest high school was in Rozet, Wyoming, in School District Three. Because the Heptner homestead was in School District Four the family would have to pay tuition to School District Three for Irene to attend the Rozet High School. Extra money was non-existent, so Frank and Laura moved the family two miles south, over the divide, to the John C. Fischer place where they would be closer to Rozet; and more importantly, they would be living in School District Three and would not have to pay tuition. Leona and her brother Oscar entered the seventh grade at Rozet. Leona and her sister and brothers rode horse-drawn vehicles (buses) to school several years before trucks were used as school buses. One of their bus drivers was Slim Whisler. Their little sister, Jeanette, joined them when, in the fall of 1927, she entered the first grade at Rozet. Alma Day was her teacher. It was in 1927 when Frank Heptner bought a new Chevrolet car.

Leona's father died in March 1928 after a series of strokes. The family continued living at the Fischer place as best they could. Her sister, Irene, graduated from high school in May. Before Irene entered Summer School at the University of Wyoming, Laura and her family traveled to Iowa in their new Chevrolet car to visit her sisters and brothers while her children became acquainted with their numerous cousins. When Oscar married Dorothy Whisler on June 5, 1929, Laura moved herself, Eugene, and Jeanette back to the homestead. Leona remained at the Fischer place with Oscar and Dorothy while she completed her senior year at Rozet High School. She graduated in May 1930. That fall she entered Normal Training at the Campbell County High School. Her teacher was Miss Clarice Clemons.

Upon completing Normal Training in the spring of 1931 Leona began looking for a teaching assignment. With the help from their long-time neighbor, Floy Jeffers, she was assigned to teach at the Cottonwood Valley School, north of the Whisler homestead on the Adon Road. While living at the Heptner homestead, she rode her favorite horses, Dandy or Brownie, every day to and from school about five miles one way.

SCHOOLS LEONA ATTENDED

COTTONWOOD SCHOOL
(1918 – 1919)

FIRST GRADE – Teacher: Edith George
Students: Irene Heptner, Eugene Heptner, Oscar Heptner, Leona Heptner,
               Gerald Woods, Bertha Woods, Lillian Woods, Winifred Hamm,
               Dorothy Hamm, Gladys Hamm, Alfred Hamm, Bessie Hamm,
               Mildred Hamm

Located: on the Charlie Woods homestead, about one mile east of the Heptner homestead.

COTTONWOOD SCHOOL
(1919 – 1920)

SECOND GRADE:
Teacher: Mark Richmond
Students: Irene Heptner, Eugene Heptner, Oscar Heptner, Leona Heptner,
              Gerald Woods, Bertha Woods, Lillian Woods, Winifred Hamm,
              Dorothy Hamm, Gladys Hamm, Alfred Hamm, Bessie Hamm,
              Mildred Hamm

Miss Florence Fair

COTTONWOOD SCHOOL
(1920 – 1921)

THIRD GRADE:

Teacher: Florence Fair

Students: Irene Heptner, Eugene Heptner, Oscar Heptner, Leona Heptner,
             Gerald Woods, Bertha Woods, Lillian Woods, Winifred Hamm,
             Dorothy Hamm, Gladys Hamm, Alfred Hamm, Bessie Hamm,
             Mildred Hamm

COTTONWOOD SCHOOL
(1921 – 1922)

FOURTH GRADE:

Teacher: Florence Stout

Students: Irene Heptner, Eugene Heptner, Oscar Heptner, Leona Heptner,
             Gerald Woods, Bertha Woods, Lillian Woods, Winifred Hamm,
             Dorothy Hamm, Gladys Hamm, Alfred Hamm, Bessie Hamm,
             Mildred Hamm

COTTONWOOD SCHOOL
(1922 – 1923)

FIFTH GRADE:
Teacher: Anne Noble
Students: Irene Heptner, Eugene Heptner, Oscar Heptner, Leona Heptner,
              Gerald Woods, Bertha Woods, Lillian Woods, Winifred Hamm,
              Dorothy Hamm, Gladys Hamm, Alfred Hamm, Bessie Hamm,
              Mildred Hamm

COTTONWOOD SCHOOL
(1923 – 1924)

SIXTH GRADE:
Teacher: Mary Weaver Nelson
Students: Irene Heptner, Eugene Heptner, Oscar Heptner, Leona Heptner,
              Gerald Woods, Bertha Woods, Lillian Woods, Winifred Hamm,
              Dorothy Hamm, Gladys Hamm, Alfred Hamm, Bessie Hamm,
              Mildred Hamm

ROZET CONSOLIDATED SCHOOL, ROZET, WYOMING
(1924 – 1925)

SEVENTH GRADE:
Teacher: Anne Morrow
Students: Partial list of students: Irene Heptner, Eugene Heptner, Oscar Heptner,
                Leona Heptner, Eileen Brennan, Laine Gardner, Ione Riley,
                Thelma Hoxsie, Joe Slattery

(Note: Eugene Heptner back row, tall boy 3rd from the left; Irene Heptner, middle of
back row, 2nd girl from left. I could not find Oscar or Leona.)

ROZET CONSOLIDATED SCHOOL, ROZET, WYOMING
(1925 – 1926)

EIGHTH GRADE:
Teacher: Belle Walker
Students: Oscar Heptner, Leona Heptner, Eileen Brennan, Laine Gardner,
                Ione Riley, Thelma Hoxsie, Joe Slattery

143

ROZET CONSOLIDATED AND HIGH SCHOOL, ROZET, WYOMING
(1926 – 1927)

ROZET SCHOOL FACALTY
Mr. Wagner, Alma Day 1-3 grades, Miss Hester 4-6 grades,
Belle Walker 7-8 grades, Anne Cameron 9-12 grades

NINETH GRADE/FRESHMAN:
Superintendent: Mr. Wagner
Teachers: Belle Walker, Anne Cameron,
Students: Oscar Heptner, Leona Heptner, Dorothy Whisler, Eileen Brennan,
                 Laine Gardner, Ione Riley, Thelma Hoxsie, Joe Slattery,
                 Richard Brennan

ROZET HIGH SCHOOL, ROZET, WYOMING
(1927 – 1928)

TENTH GRADE/SOPHOMORE:
Superintendent: Mr. Wagner
Teachers: Miss Hester, Miss Steinberg
Students: L-R: Richard *Dick* Brennan, Joe Slattery, Ione Riley, Leona Heptner, Dorothy Whisler,
               Laine Gardner, Thelma Hoxsie, Eugene Heptner, Eileen Brennan, Oscar Heptner

ROZET HIGH SCHOOL, ROZET, WYOMING
(1928 – 1929)

ELEVENTH GRADE/JUNIOR:
Superintendent: Mr. Wagner
Teachers: Harold E. Bricker, Miss M. Malsbury
Students: Eileen Brennan, Richard Brennan, Laine Gardner, Eugene Heptner, Leona Heptner,
               Oscar Heptner, Thelma Hoxsie, Ione Riley, Joe Slattery, Dorothy Whisler

145

Leona Sophia Heptner

ROZET HIGH SCHOOL, ROZET, WYOMING
(1929 – 1930)

TWELFTH GRADE/SENIOR:
Superintendent: Mr. Ernest S. Reed
Teachers: Harold E. Bricker, Miss M. Malsbury,
Students: Joseph Slattery, Leona Heptner, Eileen Brennan,
              Laine Gardner, Ione Riley, Thelma Hoxsie

SPECIAL CLASS

Lucille Butts	Louise Bricker	Jessie Baker	Jean Campbell
Norma Fitch	Eileen Foley	Rocine Garrett	Mary Gupton
Edwin George	Leona Heptner	Vivian Hamilton	Frank Hicks
	Helen McGee		

———— 1 9 3 1 ————

Leona is pictured third row, second from the left.

CAMPBELL COUNTY HIGH SCHOOL, GILLETTE, WYOMING
NORMAL TRAINING DEPARTMENT
(1930-1931

As quoted from the 1931 School Annual for Campbell County High School:

The Normal Training Department as organized in Campbell County High School, is to give training to students who will teach in rural schools in our county. There is demand for teachers in Campbell County and the department meets this need. Records show that most of the students graduating from this course have been successful in their work. The course consists of the following subjects: Psychology, Nature Study and Agriculture, Methods and Management, Major Reviews, Special Subjects and Practice Teaching.

The course is taken either the fourth or fifth years. Taken as a fifth-year course, the student has been given advanced credit at the University. A fifth-year student is usually better prepared because he (she) has had four years of Academic work and is granted thirty-six hours of credit towards an Elementary Life Certificate.

Campbell County High School gives ample opportunity for practice teaching as the department conducts a kindergarten class and a model rural schoolroom. In these two rooms, the student teachers are given the responsibility of the work under supervision. This enables them to use their own initiative and originality.

There are thirty-five students in this department this year, twenty-nine girls and six boys. Twenty will receive advanced High School Normal Training Certificates and ten will receive High School Normal Training Certificates.

Miss Neta Moran has been the assistant in the Normal Training Department this year.

On May 22, 1931, Leona was presented her Certificate of Graduation from Wyoming State High School Normal Training upon successfully completing the Wyoming State High School Normal Training Course as a fifth-year student. Her presenter was Mr. N. D. Morgan, Superintendent of Schools.

Leona always gave Miss Clarice Clemons, her Normal Training teacher, the credit for making Leona believe she, too, was fully capable of becoming a good schoolteacher. At that point in Leona's life she was sorely in need of someone who cared enough about her to gently but firmly instill confidence in her until she realized she was indeed capable of doing something as important as teaching school. Leona also had someone else in her corner, a very learned man, Mr. Floy B. Jeffers, a friend and neighbor of the family. He was on the school board for School District Four. He strongly recommended Leona for her first teaching assignment, the Cottonwood Valley School north along the Adon Road.

JEANETTE LOUISE HEPTNER

Jeanette Louise Heptner is the first Wyoming *native* in the Heptner family. She was born March 1, 1920, at home on the homestead, north of Rozet, Campbell County, Wyoming. She was the fourth daughter born to her parents Frank and Laura Heptner. Her older siblings welcomed her: Leona, age seven, Oscar, age 9, Eugene, age 11, and Irene, age 13. Her sister Leona, said she was better than a new doll. Her sisters and her brothers, proved to be good babysitters. When she got older, maybe three years old at least, her brother Eugene would take her out to the field with him. He would put her in the wagon box, and she played there until he was ready to go home with his team of horses. He would put her on the back of one of the horses and tell Jeanette to hang on to the brass horns that were a part of the neck yoke. Jeanette remembers squirming a bit because she was afraid. Her brother told her to "hang on tight to the harness, you can't fall off." Leaving the wagon in the field, he then lead the team home with Jeanette riding the horse. Before she was old enough to go to school, her sister Leona would take her to school with her. Jeanette remembers that the school kids had dug out a place in a sand bank. This was their playhouse. Jeanette can still feel Leona's arm around her as they sat in it and played. Like all sisters, Jeanette also remembers when she and Leona had a royal battle. They were visiting Obe and Mary Weaver Nelson (they were living on the Charlie Hinds place), neighbors Jeanette dearly loved to go visit. She and Leona had been sent after cattle that had strayed over the divide. Jeanette had her mother's permission to visit for a little while. After helping Leona get the cattle headed for home, Jeanette headed for Mary and Obe Nelson's house. Leona caught her and told Jeanette to get on the horse. Jeanette struggled and struggled, not wanting to get on the horse. Finally, Leona picked her up, put her on the horse and held her there. When they got home, Jeanette asked her mother about it. She looked at Jeanette, winked and smiled, and said, "I changed my mind!"

Jeanette said, "The royal battle involved me doing what I was told I could do, and Leona bound and determined to do what our mother had told her to do."

Her parents moved the family in 1924 about two miles south, over the divide, to the Fischer place to live so her sister Irene could start high school at Rozet. Jeanette entered the first grade in the fall of 1927 at Rozet Consolidated School. Alma Day was her teacher. She was the older sister of Mildred Day, who married Ton Whisler in 1930. Rex Stewart and Kathryn Ridenour were among Jeanette's classmates that first year. One of Jeanette's most vivid memories that year is that she was responsible for breaking Kathryn's nose. The children were playing *catch* while running around the schoolhouse. Jeanette changed the direction she was running and met Kathryn head-on at a corner of the schoolhouse. However, it did not damage their school friendship. Her father died on March 3, 1928, after a series of strokes. Jeanette remembers that she and Leona came down with scarletina while he was sick in bed. Their mother sent them to stay with Frank and Marna Kuehne for quite a while. At the time of her father's death, Jeanette's sister Irene was completing her twelfth grade *Senior* year at Rozet High School, graduating in May 1928. At that time her sister Leona and her brothers, Eugene and Oscar, were all in the Tenth Grade as sophomores. That summer Laura Heptner took her family on a trip, driving their new Chevrolet car to Council Bluffs, Iowa, to visit her family. There Jeanette, along with her brothers and sisters, met their Iowa cousins for the first time. When they returned to Wyoming, Irene left for Summer School at the University of Wyoming.

That September Jeanette began the second grade at Rozet, with Alma Day as her teacher once again. When Oscar married Dorothy Whisler on June 5, 1929, Jeanette's mother moved the family back to the Heptner homestead. In the fall of 1929 Jeanette began her third-grade schooling at the Woods School (formerly the Cottonwood School) with Miss Inez Stee as her teacher. Jeanette completed her third through eighth grades at the Woods School.

In September 1935, Jeanette and her mother Laura Heptner moved to Gillette. That summer her mother bought a small lot in Gillette, Wyoming, on the corner of U. S. Highway 59 and Fourth Street. Ellen Whisler also moved in with them because Jeanette and Ellen entered the Campbell County High School as freshman. They graduated on May 19, 1939. Among the 87 seniors who graduated with Jeanette and Ellen were: William Carroll, LaVern T. Harrod, and Lillian Ritter. That fall Jeanette and Ellen enrolled in the Campbell County High School Normal Training Class as fifth-year students. After graduating from Normal Training, she went to work that summer for Hank and Margaret Saunders taking care of Sally, Peggy, and Virginia from June 18 – August 17, 1940. On August 18th, she and Leona went over to their sister Irene's to help her with the dinners for the threshing crew helping Slim thresh his wheat and oats. Jeanette remembers: "I drove the car from Rozet to home. It was the first time I drove a car." Without a teaching assignment that fall, Jeanette went to work first for Mrs. Butler on April 8, 1941. She quit twelve days later, on April 20th. Then she immediately went to work for Mrs. Baird, who was ill, taking care of Mrs. Baird's twins Jane and Jean and baby sister Nancy at the Gillette Hotel. However, three days later Mrs. Baird was well, so Jeanette was again without a job. Jeanette accepted a $50.00 a month school near Recluse, but only taught there from August 29, to September 8, 1941. She accepted another teaching assignment in Crook County. Her mother and Eugene drove her to Mr. and Mrs. Charles Hauber's home on September 9, 1941. Jeanette boarded with them during her first year of teaching at the Upper Cabin Creek School.

Alma Day
Jeanette's 1st and 2nd grade teacher
at Rozet Consolidated School
Sep 1927 - May 1928
Sep 1928 - May 1919

Jeanette Louise Heptner, Age 6,
and her dog *Tootsie*
Summer 1930

Irene, Jeanette's oldest sister, one day cut and washed Jeanette's hair, helped her clean up, and then put on the best dress Jeanette had and then took her picture! No shoes. Summer was *no shoes* time. New shoes were bought only when school opened.

Tootsie was given to Jeanette by Mr. and Mrs. Winfield Cook (Floyd Cook's parents) who lived northeast of the Heptners. They brought the dog in a paper sack when Jeanette was a baby. Jeanette's mother Laura Heptner named the dog *Tootsie* after the paper sack it was delivered in, because she always referred to a paper sack/bag as a *toot*.

JEANETTE'S SCHOOL YEARS AT THE WOODS SCHOOL
(formerly the Cottonwood School)

THIRD GRADE
(1929 – 1930)

Teacher:	Miss Inez Stee
Students:	Beulah Hamm, Jeanette Heptner, June Woods, Harold Woods, Don McCune, Lester McCune

Jeanette recalls: "After the students finished their school work, Miss Stee had the girls work on learning how to sew. I made myself a pretty blue dress. Miss Stee would cut the dress out for me, and I sewed up the seams. I wore the dress on Easter Sunday at a community gathering at Frank and Marna Kuehne's home."

FOURTH GRADE
(1930 – 1931)

Teacher:	Miss Dorothy Sutherland
Students:	Beulah Hamm, Jeanette Heptner, Lester McCune, Don McCune, June Woods, and Harold Woods

During this school term Jeanette learned how to embroider. She made a set of tea towels.

FIFTH GRADE
(1931 – 1932)

Teacher: Miss Bertha Jane Anderson
Students: Jeanette Heptner, Ellen Whisler, Pauline Whisler,
             and June Woods

Jeanette recalls: "Bertha Jane Anderson taught our school as *Miss Anderson*. We found out when the school term was almost over that she was Mrs. Harold Scott. The School Board did not hire married teachers currently. So Bertha Jane and Harold kept their marriage a secret. For some reason or other, it was a thrill for her students when she finally told us her secret. Harold would come and get her on Friday. He would come into the classroom, sit in the teacher's desk, plop his feet up on her desk, boots and all, waiting for her to finish teaching for the day."

(Note: Bertha Jane and Harold were married January 31, 1932, per Mrs. Mary (McClure) Scott, their daughter-in-law 4/28/2018)

SIXTH GRADE
(1932 – 1933

Teacher: Mrs. Latham
Students: l-r: Jimmy Latham, Jeanette Heptner,
              June Woods, Pauline Whisler, and Ellen Whisler

SEVENTH GRADE
(1933 – 1934)

Alma Toro
With Betty Lou and Reva Mathews,
daughters of Manuel and Lillie (Woods) Mathews

Teacher: Alma Toro
Students: Jeanette Heptner, Ellen Whisler, Pauline Whisler,
            and June Woods

Jeanette remembers: "Alma Toro took all her students home with her to spend one night. This was a thrill. We had to sleep in the upstairs. To get upstairs we had to climb a ladder from the outside of the house. The upstairs wasn't heated. Someone heated each of us a long, flat rock. The rocks were wrapped in a blanket and tucked under our feet. It apparently was enough to keep us warm, as I don't remember being cold. Miss Toro gave me a couple more 'firsts'. She took all her students to town and fed them at a restaurant. This was the first time I had eaten at a restaurant. Then she took all of us to a movie. This was the first movie I had seen. It was a Mickey Mouse movie, with the song, 'Happy Days Are Here Again'."

(Note: Elma Toro was the daughter of John Toro, an early homesteader who was among those gentlemen who plotted out the Little Iowa Cemetery in 1917. They all were given their choices of burial plot. The Toro family moved sometime in the 1930s to Greeley, Weld County, Colorado.)

EIGHTH GRADE
(1934 – 1935)

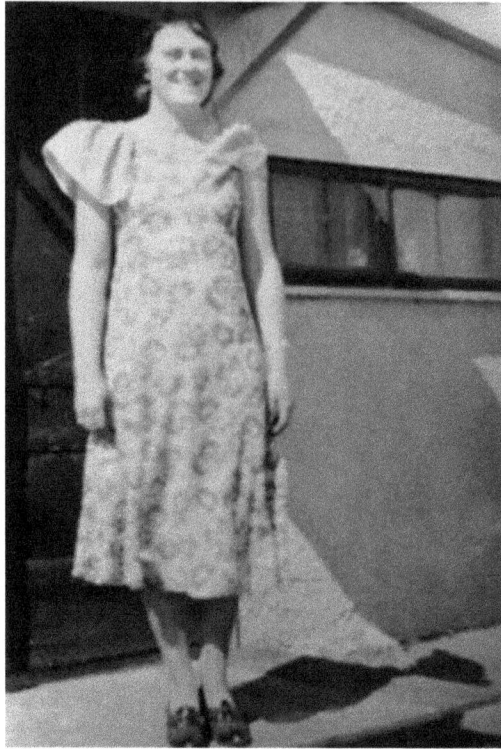

Teacher: Miss Helen Duvall
Students: Jeanette Heptner, Ellen Whisler, and Pauline Whisler

Eurith and Phil Whisler attended for a week or two at the beginning of the term then they transferred to Rozet. Miss Duvall was the daughter of Fred Duvall who homesteaded southeast of Rozet. They were not related to James Duvall who lived near them.

CERTIFICATE OF PROMOTION
THIS CERTIFIES THAT

Jeannette Heptner

having passed a satisfactory examination is this day promoted from the

eighth grade to the ninth grade in the

Course of Study prescribed for the Public Schools of this State and is

entitled to receive this Certificate of Promotion.

Given at Gillette this fifth day of June 1935

Marion Heald
County Superintendent of Schools

News Letter Publishing Co., Newcastle, Wyo.

156

CAMPBELL COUNTY HIGH SCHOOL
September 1935 – May 1939

THE CAMEL . . . 1936

FROSH

1st Row: Harl Geer, James Greer, Bill Roe, George Hunter, James Morgan, John Mulder, Tom McGee, Donald Wagner.

2nd Row: Lilith Ray, Lillian Ritter, Virginia Winter, June Spielman, Melba Fisher, Dorothy Haumann, Neva Hayden, Helen Vanderheyden, Dorothy Beaman, Octa Underwood, Wilma Hensley, Ruth Morrow, Evelyn Shults, Ruth Kinney.

3rd Row: Betty Lewis, Bessie New, Marguerite Werner, Virginia Baker, Retha Keck, Cora Glenney, Lois Harrod, Dorothy Buttes, Virginia Lamb, Jeanette Heptner, Ellenrose Littleton, June Shober, Beth Campbell, Opal Engstrom, Marian McKenzie, Bessie Dabrenz, Mamie Pearson, Carolyn Waddell, Fern Freer, June Forsha, Betty Archibald, Mary Hoblit, Mavis Rich, Ellen Whisler.

4th Row: Junior Bennick, Clovis Sanders, Joe Keeline, Donald Hayden, Robert McIntyre, Elmer Holsinger, Gale Thomas, Harold Tyrell, Leon Rich, Kenneth Hayden, Leslie Wilson, Vincent Wolff, Reginald Parnell, Gene Swarts.

5th Row: Clark McCann, Jack Reed, Ted Wright, James Williams, LeVern Harrod, Ernest Reed, Eric Ohman, Raymond Joslyn, Ben Pihlak, Tom Demos, Donald Jeffries, James Roush, James Joslyn.

Thirty-one

157

SOPHOMORES

First Row: Joe McGee, John Mulder, William Roe, Kenneth Thomas, George Hunter, Donald Wagensen, Gene Swartz, Junior Rennick, Cloris Sanders, James Morgan, Harl Geer, Donald Wagner, Donald Wilford.

Second Row: Ruth Morrow, Betty Lewis, Evelyn Shultz, Jean McKenzie, Octa Underwood, Lilith Bay, June Spielman, Lillian Ritter, Ruth Kinney, Mavis Rich, Melba Fisher, Helen Vanderhoyden, Dorothy Beaman, Neva Hayden.

Third Row: Nellie Womacks, Bessie Dolgens, Bessie New, Carolyn Waddell, Fern Freer, Dorothy Butts, Lois Harrod, Mamie Pearson, Marian MacKenzie, Virginia Lamb, Mary Lamb, Jeanette Heptner, Cora Glenney, Ellenrose Littleton, Beth Campbell, Gladys Reel, Ruby Thomas, Hazel Harris, Jane Lawson, Grace Clabaugh, Retha Keck, June Forsha, Betty Archibald, Ellen Whisler.

Fourth Row: Elmer Holsinger, Lloyd Landers, James Joslyn, Leon Rich, Wayne Rodman, Vincent Wolf, John Robinson, Eric Ohrman, Arnold Tomingas, Robert McIntyre, Archie Thomas, Raymond Joslyn, James Williams, LaVern Harrod, Clark McCann, Richard Joslyn, Tom Demos, Kenneth Haden, Ted Wright, James Roush, Ben Pihlak, Reginald Parnell, James Force, Leslie Wilson.

(Note: Jeanette is in the middle of the third row)

JUNIOR CLASS (1938)

JEANETTE HEPTNER
Humbly, like a praying nun.

ELMER HOLSINGER
Agile as a cat.

JAMES FORCE
Honest a man as ever brake
bread.

ROSALIE LEMONS
Alluring all hearts as ocean
lures the land.

SENIOR CLASS (1939)

RICHARD JOSLYN

Respectable, resolute, re-
served Richard.

Love of nature calls quiet
Richard to the fields
where he enjoys farming.

JEANETTE HEPTNER

Judicious, just, justifiable
Jeanette.

Reserve and practical ex-
perience will aid Jeanette
in her teaching career.

HAZEL HARRIS

Hospitable, humble, hearty
Hazel.

Energetic Hazel is known
and recognized for great
athletic prowess.

HARL GEER

Hopeful, harmonica-playing,
Hazy Harl.

Carefree Harl gives a
smile of approval to any-
thing that is fun.

20

COMMENCEMENT EXERCISES

CAMPBELL COUNTY HIGH SCHOOL

HIGH SCHOOL GYMNASIUM, 8:00 P. M.
FRIDAY, MAY 19, 1939

PROGRAM

Program Chairman..E. R. Pines
Secretary of the Campbell County High School Board

Processional, Glorious Youth..................High School Orchestra

Invocation......................................Reverend T. L. Sharrah

Clarinet Quartette, Twilight—Reynard..............................
Marion Sharrah, Helen Louise Daly, Donovan Reilly, Lois Dickey

Salutation...Ruth Morrow

Commencement Address...........................Dr. A. G. Crane
President of the University of Wyoming

Vocal Solo, O! Dry Those Tears—Del Riego......LaVern Harrod

Valediction...Dorothy Butts

Presentation of Normal Training Diplomas....Miss Blanche Kelly
Head of the Normal Department

Presentation of Diplomas and Scholarships.......R. B. Marquiss
President of the Campbell County High School Board

Benediction..................................Reverend V. G. Lewis

Selection..................................High School Orchestra

---

CLASS OF 1939

Allen, Norma Irene
Archibald, Elizabeth
Baker, Virginia
Beaman, Dorothy Juanita
Bennick, Junior L.
Birdsall, Betty
Brandner, Betty L.
Bricker, Edna
Burr, Charles E.
Butts, Dorothy
Camblin, DeLaine
Carroll, William E.
Clabaugh, Grace Carol
Coyle, Patty
Deaver, Robert M.
Demos, Tom, Jr.
Dillon, Samuel A.
Ferguson, Ellen Rose L.
Force, James G.
Forsha, June
Freer, Fernie M.
Galbreath, Loraine
Geer, Harl G.
Gibson, Mary Gayl
Glessey, Cora
Greer, Charles, Jr.
Haden, Kenneth E.
Harrod, LaVern T.
Harrod, Lois

Hausmann, Dorothy M.
Hayden, Neva M.
Hayden, Donald A.
Heptner, Jeanette Louise
Holsinger, Elmer, Jr.
Hunter, George E.
Jensen, Laura W.
Jones, Frances R.
Joslyn, Raymond W.
Joslyn, Richard J.
Keck, Retha June
Kinney, Ruth Jane
Landers, Lloyd
Lewis, Betty
MacKenzie, Marian
McCann, Clark
McGee, Tom W.
McKenzie, Jean
Matheny, Ruby
Morrow, Ruth E.
Mosebar, Marion A.
Mulder, John E., Jr.
New, Bessie E.
Ohman, Eric J.
Osborn, Harvey C.
Parnell, Reginald
Rich, Mavis
Ritter, Lillian M.
Robinson, John W.
Rodman, T. Wayne

Roe, George William
Roush, James W.
Scott, Aleta I.
Sharrah, Marion
Shellenbarger, Kathryn Louise
Shultz, Joyce
Sinclair, Pete J.
Spielman, June
Swartz, Gene
Taft, Ramona Willmetta
Thomas, Archie G.
Thomas, Gale
Thomas, Ruby W.
Thompson, Marjorie E.
Tomingas, Arnold
Tomingas, Henry R.
Underwood, Octa
Vanderheyden, Helen Lucille
Waddell, Carolyn Mae
Wagenson, Donald W.
Wagner, Donald G.
Wenande, Nellie
Whisler, Ellen Jean
Williford, Donald Richard
Wilkinson, Mary Beth
Williams, James
Wilson, Leslie
Wocicki, Leota A.
Wright, Theodore Otis

Class Flower: Yellow Rose   Class Colors: Black and Gold
Class Motto: We Undertake $2B^2$

160

Jeanette Louise Heptner
Class of 1939
Campbell County High School
Gillette, Wyoming

Ellen Joan Whisler
Class of 1939
Campbell County High School
Gillette, Wyoming

PART THREE

THE TEACHING YEARS

(1931 - 1977)

Miss Heptner

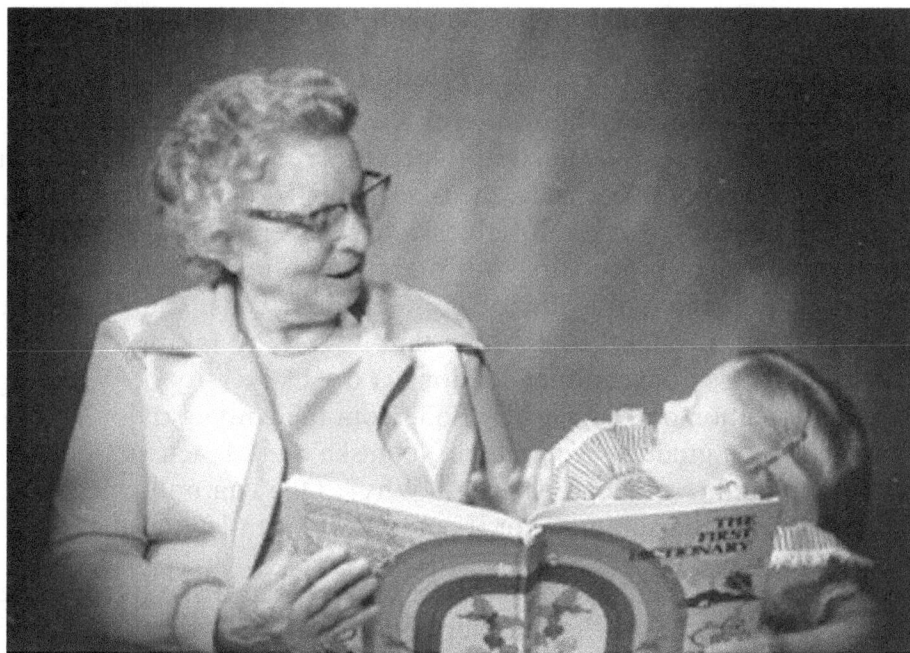

Leona Heptner with Allyson Sicks
(about 1980)

LEONA SOPHIA HEPTNER
(Teaching Years 1931 – 1975)

Leona's first teaching assignment, at age 19, was at the Cottonwood Valley School in September 1931. The school was located near the Perry Wallace homestead about six miles northwest of the Heptner homestead along the Adon Road. Her first students were Ruth Wallace, Lee Wallace, Ted Wallace, Gertrude *Gertie* Hartzell, and Bernard White. She taught there for three years. Leona lived at home and rode a horse daily to and from school. She took turns riding Dandy and Brownie. Leona remembered clearly that first glorious September morning she rode toward the schoolhouse. She wondered and wondered how things would be that first day of teaching. "Would the kids be ready to go to school? Would they mind me? Would they even be willing to come into the school when I rang the school bell? How good I felt when they didn't give me any trouble at all and we had a most wonderful school day. This was a happy beginning of my many years as a teacher of elementary school children in Campbell County, Wyoming."

When Leona began teaching in 1931 she was required to renew her teaching certificate every three years. A new certificate would only be issued if she earned nine credit hours during those three years. In addition to full time teaching, she accomplished this requirement by attending summer school at the University of Wyoming, Laramie, Wyoming, the Black Hills Teachers College, Spearfish, South Dakota, and the Nebraska State Teachers College, Chadron, Nebraska, whenever she could. Then in 1951, the Wyoming State Department of Education began proceedings to establish the regulation that all schoolteachers must have college degrees. Quickly Leona and a few of her teacher friends, Carolyn Oedekovan, and Hertha Semlek among others, began working hard to achieve that degree by taking extension courses at night, correspondence lessons, and going to the summer sessions at the University of Wyoming. She received her Bachelor of Arts Degree in Education on August 21, 1953, from the University of Wyoming. In the summer of 1956, Leona and Jeanette began graduate work at the Nebraska State Teachers College, Chadron, Nebraska. However, Leona did not complete her graduate studies. Why? One can only speculate. It is possible that she was needed at the ranch during the summers, or it could have been lack of money.

In 1946 when Leona began teaching in the Gillette Grade School she lived in the same house on the corner of Fourth and U. S. Highway 59 that her mother bought in 1935 when her sister Jeanette began high school. In the late 1950s Leona's brothers began building her a new house between her house and Irene and Slim Whisler's home. Slim and Irene had bought one half of the lot in 1951 to put a small house on for the same reason Laura Heptner bought the original lot—Lorna was attending Campbell County High School. Leona lived in her new house until aout 1973/4 when the Gillette City Council rezoned that part of the city as commercial property. Leona went looking for another house to live in. She found a house at 412 Circle Drive, a street behind the Farmer's Co-Op, and moved in.

During the summers that Leona and Jeanette were not attending summer school they helped their brother Eugene at the ranch; planting a garden, canning vegetables from that garden, cooking for themselves, the inevitable cousins visiting from Iowa, or their nieces Lorna and Olive from Virginia, and the hay crews that included his brother Oscar and nephew Darrell along with young men Eugene hired for the summer to help put up hay. The three of them would, when time allowed, go fishing in the Big Horn Mountains or the Jigg's Reservoir that Eugene had built over the hill north of the ranch. Another favorite pastime the three enjoyed was playing cards with their old neighbor Eunice Ranney and other friends old and new.

During her teaching years Leona pursued and became involved with other interests outside of her teaching:

On January 12, 1947, she became a member of the First Presbyterian Church on Carey Avenue just across the street from the Gillette Grade School. The Reverend L. V. Osborne was the Pastor. She served as a Deacon and as an Elder and served on many committees. She is a member of the United Presbyterian Women (UPW) of the church and a faithful member of its Bible Study Circle.

Leona joined the Jewel Rebekah Lodge No. 28, on December 12, 1951. Its members and the fellowship she found with them became a very important part of Leona's life outside of the classroom. After serving in several positions she was installed in 1976 as Noble Grand. On December 16, 1976, she received her twenty-five year Jewel from the Jewel Rebekah Lodge No. 28. In 1980, she was elected as Treasurer, a position she served in until the year 2000 when due to poor health she resigned that position. In 1987-1989 Leona served as President of the Northeast Wyoming Rebekah District No. 8. This District includes Rebekah Lodges from Sundance, Newcastle, Upton, and Gillette. Leona and her sister, Jeanette, were honored on November 13, 1988, by the Jewel Rebekah Lodge No. 28, with the Decoration of Chivalry, the highest honor given by this Lodge.

In November 1957 Leona became a member of the Theta Chapter, Delta Kappa Gamma Society International. She remained active in this chapter until her health prevented her from participating. She served in all the offices and served as President for two terms and has chaired or worked on most of the committees. She especially enjoyed attending the state conferences where she shared her teaching ideas with other teachers as they learned about new methods for teaching.

On June 7, 1979, she joined the Pythians, Pythagoras Temple No. 8, in Gillette, Wyoming.

Leona was also a member of the Stitch and Skillet Club, a Campbell County Extension homemakers club, and the Past Nobel Grand's Club. She was also a dedicated supporter of the Campbell County Senior Citizens Center where she took lessons in oil painting. Her paintings have won prizes at both the Campbell County Fair and the Wyoming State Fair.

Having a lifetime of love for children, Leona became instrumental in providing support for the Yellowstone Boys and Girls Ranch, at Billings, Montana, and the Cathedral Children's Home in Laramie, Wyoming. She visited these two special places many times. As she talked with the children living there she observed how her support had helped these institutions move children out of desperate and unsafe home situations; teaching them how to live in the world using the skills developed in these homes.

Leona's hobbies were: reading, playing cards, crocheting, knitting, tatting, oil painting, and other crafts.

Leona retired from teaching at the end of the 1974-1975 school term after forty-five years. She taught, except for one school term in Crook County, all her years in Campbell County. She went from one room rural schools to the modern school systems provided in the 1970s. Her experiences during the early years provided her with great determination to do the best she could under any circumstances. Approximately eight hundred children passed through her school rooms—mostly first graders. Leona especially loved teaching her first graders and took immense pride in their accomplishments as adults. She made many lifelong friends among her fellow rural and city school teachers. However, and more importantly, she enjoyed the friendship of her students many of whom still lived in Campbell County.

Her wish, during the *golden retirement* years, was that children everywhere could grow up enjoying their schooling and then using what they learn to enjoy their life's work as much as she had. It is this love for children, her ready smile, and her ever ready helping hand that became her trademark.

Leona beside the little house she rented
at Rozet behind the post office when she was teaching
First and Second Grades at Rozet Consolidated Schools.
(About 1941)

Jeanette and Leona (Cowgirls)
On Grandma Heptner's lot
East of Gillette
(About July 1937)

Leona on the Heptner Place
Type of car unknown
Late 1930s

Leona and Jeanette (other lady unknown) in their garden;
Eugene's combine in background
looking south to the eastern portion of the divide
1960

Leona's 2nd avocation was hair dresser.
Here she is giving her good friend,
Hertha (Semlek) Larsen, a *perm.*
1969

Leona feeding the chickens – 1940s

Leona milking *Old Jersey*
(About 1954)

Leona feeding the ranch geese – 1965
Building in upper right is remnants of the old ice house

Ronnie Joslyn, *the summer help*, Leona, Jeanette, and Eugene
taking a ride in 1960 on Jigg's Reservoir that he built

NOON DINNER BREAK FOR THE HAYING CREW AND ONE VISITING NIECE
Summer 1963
Oscar Heptner, _____, Leona Heptner, Darrell Heptner,
Jeff Cummings (Oscar's nephew and Darrell and Lorna's cousin
from Basin, Wyoming), Jeanette Heptner, and Eugene Heptner

Leona's new house at 4th Street east of the Douglas Highway
that Eugene and Oscar built for her.

412 Circle Drive, Gillette, Wyoming
Winter 1975

(Note: This photo is two pictures spliced together.)

LEONA'S TEACHING ASSIGNMENTS AND SALARIES

TERMS	SCHOOL	SALARY
1931 – 1932	Cottonwood Valley	720.00
1932 – 1933	Cottonwood Valley	700.00
1933 – 1934	Cottonwood Valley	600.00
1934 – 1935	Deer Creek	595.00
1935 – 1936	Calf Creek	600.00
1936 – 1937	Woods	600.00
1937 – 1938	Woods	600.00
1938 – 1939	Rozet Consolidated	765.00
1939 – 1940	Rozet Consolidated	765.00
1940 – 1941	Rozet Consolidated	765.00
1941 – 1942	Rozet Consolidated	765.00
1942 – 1943	Rozet Consolidated	765.00
1943 – 1944	Rozet Consolidated	850.00
1944 – 1945	West End (Crook County)	850.00
1945 – 1946	Rozet Consolidated	935.00
1946 – 1947	Gillette Grade School	1,280.00
1947 – 1948	Gillette Grade School	1,820.00
1948 – 1949	Gillette Grade School	2,340.00
1949 – 1950	Gillette Grade School	2,520.00
1950 – 1951	Gillette Grade School	2,680.00
1951 – 1952	Gillette Grade School	2,760.00
1952 – 1953	Gillette Grade School	3,060.00
1953 – 1954	Gillette Grade School	3,420.00
1954 – 1955	Gillette Grade School	3,540.00
1955 – 1956	Gillette Grade School	3,660.00
1956 – 1957	Gillette Grade School	3,780.00
1957 – 1958	Gillette Grade School	4,020.00
1958 – 1959	Gillette Grade School	4,500.00
1959 – 1960	Gillette Grade School	4,740.00
1960 – 1961	Gillette Grade School	4,860.00
1961 – 1962	Gillette Grade School	5,160.00
1962 – 1963	Gillette Grade School	5,580.00
1963 – 1964	Gillette Grade School	5,580.00
1964 – 1965	Gillette Grade School	6,204.00
1965 – 1966	Gillette Grade School	6,722.00
1966 – 1967	Gillette – Westside Elementar	6,800.00
1967 – 1968	Gillette – Westside Elementary	7,000.00
1968 – 1969	Gillette – Westside Elementary	7,500.00
1969 – 1970	Gillette – Westside Elementary	9,600.00
1970 – 1971	Gillette – Westside Elementary	12,137.00
1971 – 1972	Gillette – Westside Elementary	12,830.00
1972 – 1973	Gillette – Westside Elementary	12,830.00
1973 – 1974	Gillette – Westside Elementary	13,005.00
1974 – 1975	Gillette – Westside Elementary	14,385.00
1975 -	RETIREMENT	

COTTONWOOD VALLEY SCHOOL
(1931 – 1932)

Brownie

One of Leona's favorite sources of transportation to school
She took turns riding Brownie and Dandy

Students: Leone Donner
              Gertrude *Gertie* Hartzell
              Ruth Wallace
              Lee Wallace
              Ted Wallace
              Dean Whisler
              Bernard White

Salary: $720.00

COTTONWOOD VALLEY SCHOOL
(1932 – 1933)

Dandy
Leona's favorite source of transportation to school
She took turns riding Dandy and Brownie

Students: June Donner
Leone Donner
Lee Wallace
Ted Wallace
Dean Whisler

Salary: $700.00

COTTONWOOD VALLEY SCHOOL
(1933 – 1934)

Cottonwood Valley and Deer Creek Schools Picnic
Spring 1934

Back Row: Lee Wallace, Leona Heptner, Gladys Weaver
Front Row: June and Leone Donner, Ted Wallace, Dean Whisler,
             Alvina Weaver, Mary Hanslip (Leonard Whisler missing)

Salary: $600.00

DEER CREEK SCHOOL
(1934 – 1935)

Miss Heptner
1935

Students: Mary Hanslip
               Alvina Weaver
               Johnny Weaver
               Dean Whisler
               Leonard Whisler

Salary: $595.00

CALF CREEK SCHOOL
(1935 – 1936)

Students:	Polly Spangler, Everett Spangler,
	Wilma McGee, Carl McGee,
	Phyllis Fulton, Shirley Teagle,
	Lena Thorp

Salary: $600.00

This school was located north of Gillette off the Wyoming highway 14-16. Leona stayed at Bob Johnson's in their former cabin. It came furnished complete with a cook stove in which Leona baked bread on weekends. Helen Duvall also boarded with Leona in the Johnson cabin.

Bob Johnson was the engineer involved with the construction of the new Rozet School and Gym that was made of black cinder-rock.

WOODS SCHOOL
(Formerly the Cottonwood School)
(1936 – 1937)

(No photo available)

Students: Margaret Riecken
                _____ Riecken (brother)
                Pauline Whisler
                Evelyn Whisler

Salary: $$600.00

WOODS SCHOOL
(1937 – 1938)

Students: Darleen Heptner
               Betty Mathews

Salary: $600.00

Leona with Darleen,
Darrell, and Shirley
1937

Miss Heptner

ROZET CONSOLIDATED AND HIGH SCHOOL
SCHOOL DISTRICT THREE
ROZET, CAMPBELL COUNTY, WYOMING
Leona taught 1st and 2nd grades from fall 1938 – spring 1944

PRIMARY GRADES (FIRST AND SECOND)

Students:

Back Row: Robert Prazma, Larry Beck, Miss Heptner, Kenneth Burr, Billy Nelson, and Allen Whisler

Front Row: Danny Beck, Verlin Duvall, Nadine Duvall, Phyllis Peterson, _____, and Harold Ridenour

Salary: $765.00

ROZET CONSOLIDATED SCHOOL
(1939 – 1940)

PRIMARY GRADES (FIRST AND SECOND)

Students:

    Back Row: Darrell Heptner, Harold Ridenour, Allen Whisler, and Verlin Duvall

    Front Row: Jerry Prazma, Nadine Duvall, Phyllis Peterson, Curtis Burr, and Miss Heptner

(Not pictured above: Jimmy Misch)

Salary: $765.00

Jimmy Misch and his little brother

ROZET CONSOLIDATED SCHOOL
(1940 – 1941)

PRIMARY GRADES (FIRST AND SECOND)

Students:

    Back Row: _____, Darrell Heptner, Jerry Prazma, Curtis Burr, Miss Heptner

    Front Row: Edna Thompson, Nadine Duvall, Pauline Burr, and Elsie Olson

Salary: $765.00

ROZET CONSOLIDATED SCHOOL
(1941 – 1942)

PRIMARY GRADES (FIRST AND SECOND)

Students: Emma Brunson, Elsie Olsen, Norma Peterson, Pauline Burr,
Donald Scott, Miss Heptner, Edna Thompson, Shirley Heptner,
_____, Jerry Harrod, and Dorothy Grey

Salary: $765.00

ROZET CONSOLIDATED SCHOOL
(1942 – 1943)

PRIMARY GRADES (FIRST AND SECOND)

Students:
    Back Row: Donnie Whisler, Johnny Duvall, Lorna Whisler, and Dorothy Grey

    Front Row: Miss Heptner, Shirley Heptner, Emma Brunson, Betty Gray, Janice Day, and Nadine Brennan

Salary: $765.00

ROZET, WYO   GRADES 1-2-3   1944

PRIMARY GRADES (FIRST, SECOND, THIRD)

Students:

Back Row: Johnny Duvall, Nadine Brennan, Janice Day,
              Damon Reel, and Miss Heptner
Front Row: Sally Whisler, Jackie Fittrol, Phyllis Johnson,
              and Rosa Ridenour

Salary: $850.00

WEST END SCHOOL
CROOK COUNTY, WYOMING
(1944 – 1945)

Miss Heptner and Bonnie, Norma, Betty, and Deloris Pollack

This school was located just across the Crook County Line about one mile east of the Pleasant Valley Cemetery on Miller Creek Road.

Salary: $850.00

Combined *End-of-the-Year* Picnic - 1945
West End School, Crook County, Wyoming; teacher Leona Heptner
Whisler School, Campbell County, Wyoming; teacher Jeanette Heptner

Adults - Back Row: Marie Dillinger, Leona Heptner, Jeanette Heptner
Children - Front Row: Ed Dillinger, Alan *Bud* Dillinger, Judy Hatfield, Maxine Dillinger,
Betty, Bonnie, and Deloris Pollock, Deloris Whisler, Barbara Whisler, Lorna Whisler, Donnie Whisler

ROZET CONSOLIDATED SCHOOL
(1945 – 1946)

PRIMAY GRADES (FIRST, SECOND, THIRD)

Students:

Back Row: Miss Heptner and Carol Potter

Middle Row: Damon Reel, Jackie Fittrol, Rosa Ridenour, Joann Uhl, and Jimmy Brennan

Front Row: Winfred Brunson, Nancy Whisler, Jerry Brennan, Wilma Thar, and Teddy Fittrol

Salary: $935.00

GILLETTE GRADE SCHOOL
(1946 – 1966)

Fourth Street and Carey Avenue
Gillette, Wyoming

GILLETTE GRADE SCHOOL
(1946 – 1947)
Fourth Grade
Salary: $1,280.00

FOURTH GRADE CLASS

Students: Back Row: Raymond Record, Bobby Wenger, Robert Haley, Eugene Faas, Donald Hermann, David Christensen, Jerry McManamen, Sammy Christensen, Richard James, Harold Edwards, Donnie Carlton, Jimmy Record, Ronnie Lynde, Donnie Freer, Orville Noldner, Frankie Shippy

Middle Row: Robert Bridwell, Bobby Lou Cohee, Iris Small, Jean Ann Matheson, Ann Watt, Mary Niswender, Iva Kay Hedlund, Wanda Harper, Deanna Gaddis, Mellissa Hughes, Emma Lou Hedlund.

Front Row: Joe Norfolk, Dan Watt, Jimmy Eldridge, Raymond Lane, Virl Ewing, Bobby Shipley, Tommy Tilson

GILLETTE GRADE SCHOOL
(1947 – 1948)
First Grade
Salary: $1,820.00

(List of students' names missing)

GILLETTE GRADE SCHOOL
(1948 – 1949)
First Grade
Salary: $2,340.00

Names of Students

Beverly Jean Bennett
Larry Wayne Bray
James Brewer
Ann Laura Burns
Sandra Lee Christman
Dickie Cullins
Mildred Jule Frederick
Bonnie Ruth Harlow
Lee Harrod
Priscilla Elaine Hathaway
Glen Irvin Hayden
Thomas Heinbaugh
Bette Holcomb
Leonard Hunt
Thomas James

Floyd Jaramillo
Reba Ann Maddox
Sheila Joan McCalla
Donald Ray McMahand
Ronald Jay McMahand
Johnny Mooney
Camille Norfolk
Michael O'Connell
Karen Diane Parsons
Juanita Slates
Neta Jo Smelser
Jimmy Sutherland
Sharon Thompson
Claudette Weese

GILLETTE GRADE SCHOOL
(1949 – 1950)
First Grade
Salary: $2,520.00

(List of students' names missing)

GILLETTE GRADE SCHOOL
(1950 – 1951)
Salary: $2,680.00

Boys

Girls

(List of students' names missing)

GILLETTE GRADE SCHOOL
(1951 – 1952)
Salary: $2,760.00

Miss Heptoor   Judy Drake   Carol Wilkinson   Cindy Hughes   Jeanette Eldridge

Carol Holloman   Susan Saunders   Vickey Solomon   Joan Hopper   Carol Edmondson

(Note: Leona made this little booklet as a present for each child at the end of the school year)

Dixie Mooney   Danny Baumfalk   Judy Brewer   Jimmy Nisselius   Karen Perkins

Terry Mapel   Toby Thompson   Bud Shane   Tommy Oliver   Edwin Harrod

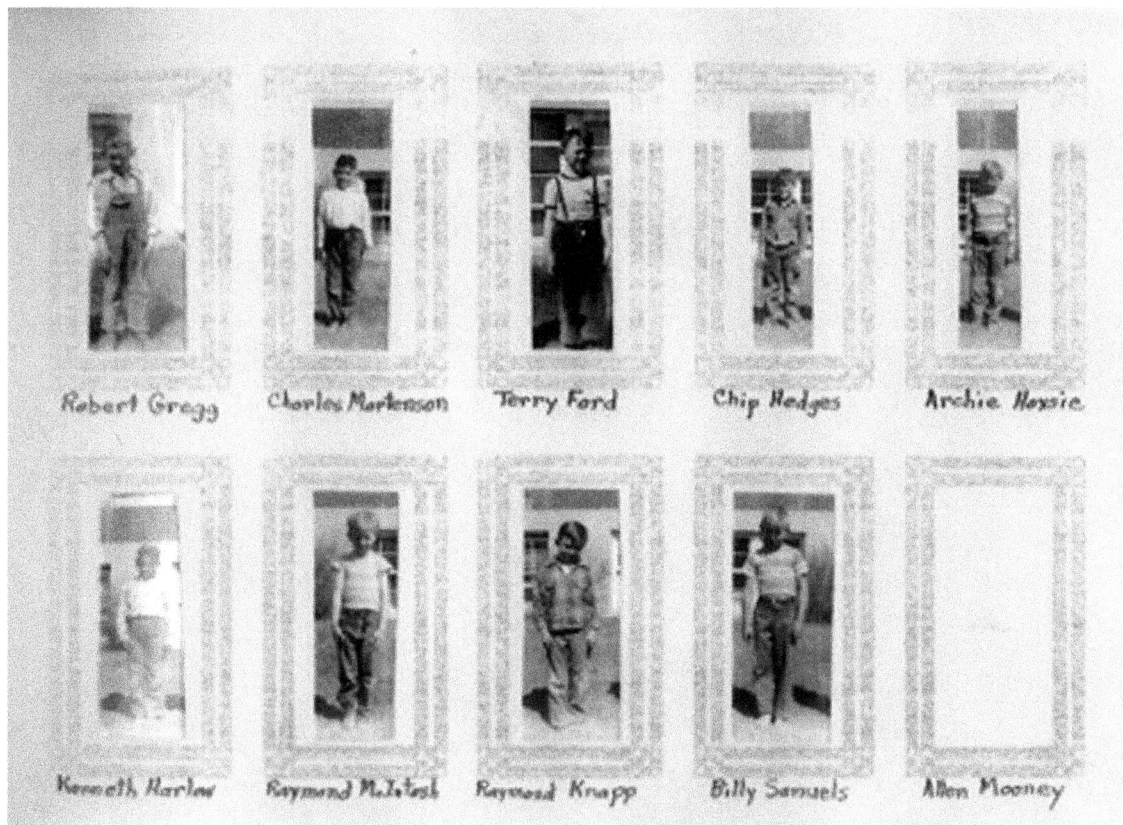

Robert Gregg   Charles Markenson   Terry Ford   Chip Hedges   Archie Hoxsie

Kenneth Harlow   Raymond McIntosh   Raymond Knapp   Billy Samuels   Allen Mooney

GILLETTE GRADE SCHOOL
(1952 – 1953)
First Grade
Salary: $3,060.00

(List of students' names missing)

(Note: Guy Cook first in kneeling row)

GRADUATED WITH A BACHILOR DEGREE IN EDUCATION
UNIVERSITY OF WOMING
Aug 21, 1953

Leona Sophia Heptner

The University of Wyoming

College of Education

Know all men by these presents, That

Leona Sophia Heptner

having completed the Course of Study prescribed by the Faculty for this College of the University, and having complied with all other requirements for graduation therefrom, has therefore been granted the degree of

Bachelor of Arts

In Testimony Whereof, this Diploma has been granted, attested with the Seal of the University and with the Signatures of its duly authorized officers at Laramie, Wyoming, this 21st day of August, in the year of our Lord nineteen hundred fifty-three.

PRESIDENT OF THE BOARD OF TRUSTEES   PRESIDENT OF THE UNIVERSITY

SECRETARY OF THE BOARD OF TRUSTEES   DEAN

GILLETTE GRADE SCHOOL
(1953 – 1954)
First Grade
Salary: $3,430.00

Student	Father/Mother	Occupation
Donald Edward Allen	Connie Allen	baker
Linda Laree Appley	Judson Appley	truck driver
Gay Diane Bennick	J. L.Bennick	bank teller
Jance Lea Brewer	L.O. Brewer	Supt of Schools
Sandra Jeanne Burr	Leslie Alwyn Burr	mechanic
Ladeana Bell Carlton	Mrs. Florence Carlton	
Andrew Linscott Charlson	Archer Andrew Charlson	Hi-way Dept
George Czapskie	Harold Rank	plumber
Lonnie Dale Dickinson	Kenneth Dickinson	radio repair
Steven George Dorrington	George Dorrington	teacher
Robert Harold Ernst	C. R. Ernst	printer
Bonnie Ray Frisbee	Bob Leftus	
Richard Lee Hensley	Jack Hensley	Hi-way service
Catherine May Hughes	Henry A. Hughes	Const. Worker
James Ronald Joslyn	James Vincent Joslyn	body shop
Kenneth Hume Kerr, Jr.	Kenneth Hume, Sr.	Vet. Ins.
Peggy Jo Knapp	Leslie Ray Knapp	baker
Benny Wayne Lara	Benerito Lara	Const. worker
Michael Alvin Manor	Alvin Manor	Const. worker

GILLETTE GRADE SCHOOL
(1953 – 1954)
First Grade (Continued)

Student	Father/Mother	Occupation
Gregory Lewis Marsh	Delmer Marsh	welder
Elinar Matheson	Edward Matheson	pensioner
James Douglas McCalla	Rosco McCalla	Record Motor
Kathleen Elaine McLaughlin	Alva George McLaughlin	City Employee
Katherine McLaughlin	Alva George McLaughlin	City Employee
Jeanie Raye Miller	Willard Eugene Miller	Driller
James Donald Noecker	LeRoy Noecker	shoemaker
Beverly Okray	Maurice Okray	undersheriff
Michael Harold Samuels	Harold Samuels	tourist court
Mary Linda Tarver	Stephen Tarver	public accountant
Donna Jeanne Vaught	William Leroy Vaught	Soil Conservation
Debra Walker	Robert Walker	Surveyor
Sally Jan Walker	Howard Walker	laborer
Jeffrey Church Wenckus	Stanley B. Wenckus	jeweler
Donna June Wolf	James Dillon Wolf	welder

GILLETTE GRADE SCHOOL
(1954 – 1955)
First Grade
Salary: $3,540.00

(No class photo available)

Student	Father/Mother	Occupation
Vivian Ann Addison	Russell Addison	Hi-way Department
Nancy Lee Allen	Connie Allen	baker
Margo Ann Bennick	Jack Bennick	bank
Nancy Jean Bertoncely	Peter Bertoncely, Jr	motel
Mark Andrew Cameron	Andrew Cameron	minister
Linda May Conway		
Christina Carlon	Tom E. Carlon	carpenter
Linda Jean Dahlman	Dutch Dahlman	Gambles Store
Edward Wayne Eldridge	Wayne Eldridge	shovel operator
John Alan Forsha	Bill Forsha	Forsha Service
Dennis Tyler Hall	Corder Hall	Ray Oil Co.
Michael Howard Hanson	Milford Hanson	bakery
Susan Myrtle Harlow	Kenneth Harlow	trucker
George Alex Henson, Jr.	George Henson	oil crew
Emina Hodgzic	Eigo Hodzic	carpenter
Michael Lyn Hughes	Woodie Hughes	R & R Supply
Diane Lee Johnson	Vernon Johnson	
Terry Lee Jones	William C. Jones	painter
Robert Michael Kennedy	Tom Kennedy	teacher
William Ross Kielty	Richard L. Kielty	R. H. Ray
Anna Marie Klug	Mark Klug	Army Instr.
Donnie Ray Lara	Ben and Rose Lara	laborer
Ella Mae Levison	Howard E. Levison	mechanic
Larry Francis Linneman	Henry F. Linneman	hospital attendent
Gary Wayne Marsh	George Marsh, Jr	Hested Store
Clifford Herbert Massie, Jr	Clifford H. Massie, Sr.	Self-employed
Marie Louise McMahon	Tom McMahon	post office
Johnetta Lou Minser	John G. Minser	teacher
Beverly Oliver	Wayne Oliver	
Joe Ernest Record	Clarence Record	R & R Supply
Lewis Clifton Reed	Ernest Reed	carpenter
George Ernst Rush	William E. Rush	mechanic
Charles Ray Shoemaker	Charles Shoemaker	Army (Reserve)
Carol Ann Sorenson	Albert Sorenson	movie theater
Judy K. Taylor	Norris Taylor	filling station
Roberta Dalene Tyrrell	Lee O. Tyrrell	post office
Barbara Kay Williams	Richard C. Baughman (step)	doctor

GILLETTE GRADE SCHOOL
(1955 – 1956)
First Grade
Salary: $3,660.00

School Days 55-56   School Days 55-56   School Days 55-56   School Days 55-56

School Days 55-56   School Days 55-56   School Days 55-56   School Days 55-56

School Days 55-56   School Days 55-56   ool Days 55-56   School Days 55-56

School Days 55-56   School Days 55-56   School Days 55-56   School Days 55-56

First Grade (1955 – 1956) continued

School Days 55-56

School Days 55-56

Karan

School Days 55-56

School Days 55-56

School Days 55-56

School Days 55-56

School Days 55-56

School Days 55-56

School Days 55-56

School Days 55-56

School Days 55-56

School Days 55-56

School Days 55-56

School Days 55-56

School Days 55-56

School Days 55-56

School Days 55-56

206

GILLETTE GRADE SCHOOL
(1955 – 1956)
First Grade (Continued)

Student Enrollment

Robert Dean Albertson
Kathleen Marie Berg
Robert Ervin Brown
Sharon Diane Burr
Cynthia Burton
Calvin Gene Darnall
Thomas Martin Demos
Shirley Ann Dyer
Gary Lee Ekis
James Eyre
Gayl D'Ann Fischer
Judy Elaine Fischer
Timothy Francis Fleck
Zana Kay Fox
Kathleen Marie Hardy
Joseph Michael Hays
Virginia Louise Hillman
Cheri Lee Holbert
Mary Josephine Joslyn
Karen Lee Kane
Thomas Kyte
Michael Thomas Looby
James William Lubken
Robert R. Mackey
Gloria Sue Matlack
Mary Linda Mays
Kathleen Theresa McMahon
Doris Grace Rhoads
Richard Allen Sack
James Francis Shippy
Dalene Grace Snearly
William John Spangler
Steve Edwin Spears
Gary Lee Spoering
Lynn LaRae Spracklin
James Eldon Tholson
Charles Arlan Tyrrell
Ralph Neil West
William Frederick Wintermute

GILLETTE GRADE SCHOOL
(1956 – 1957)
First Grade
Salary: $3,780.00

(No class photo available)

Student Enrollment	Parents
Robert Albertson	Mrs. Geary Davis
Joe Archuleta	Max and Anita Archuleta
Orlando Archuleta	Max and Anita Archuleta
Allan Ray Baughman	Richard C. and Mable Baughman
Denise Marie Burney	Ollie and Hazel Burney
Thomas George Carlon	Tom and Phyllis Carlon
Dalene Marie Fischer	Chuck and Mary Fischer
Richard Marion George	Jack and Jean George
Donna Rae Hardy	Howard and Kathleen Hardy
Sarah Jane Hart	M. L. Hart
James Learns Hays	Robert and Betty Hays
Johanna Marie Hotlinger	Duane Hotlinger
Steven Gregory Howe	George and Althea Howe
Clark Izzard	Clark and Jean Izzard
Burke Louis Jackson	Kenneth and Marjorie Jackson
Linda Lee Jones	Glenn and Fannie Jones
Susan Marie Keeline	Joe, Jr. and Pauline Keeline
Caroline Beryl Kenitzer	Norman and Deloris Kenitzer
William Kenneth Lara	Ben and Rosa Lara
Leonard G. Marsh	George and Dorothy Marsh
Mary Jane Niswender	Olie and Pauline Niswender
James Hugh Scott	Bernard and Mary Scott
Terry Allen Sparks	Bob and Anna Rose Rourke
David Lee Stephenson	Hervis and Thora Stephenson
Priscilla Ann Tarver	Stephan and Ruth Tarver
Nicki Dayle Verley	James L and Mary Jean Verley
Jeanne Kay Workman	Clifton and Phyllis Workman

GILLETTE GRADE SCHOOL
(1957 – 1958)
First Grade
Salary: $4,020.00

GILLETTE SCHOOL -GRADE 1 - 1957-58

Student Enrollment	Parents
Linnie Vondean Addison	Russell and Vivian Addison
Nicky Lynn Anderson	John and Betty Lou Anderson
Robert Frank Bailey	Frank and Sybil Bailey
Cynthia Anne Bates	Richard and Gertrude Bates
Nancy Lee Bell	John and Barbara Bell
Charlotte Roseann Bills	Herbert and Rosemarie Bills
Cathleen Phyllis Carlon	Tom Carlon and Phyllis Wolff
Renee Ellen Darnell	Lloyd and Lola Darnell
Robert Dorsey Downes	Robert and Alice Downes
Douglas Arden Drovdal	Norris and Norma Drovdal
Carol Dee Eddy	Lonnie and Betty Eddy
Thomas Allen Edmunds	Alfred and Ruth Mae Edmunds
Anita Lynn Fischer	Henry and Evelyn Fischer

GILLETTE GRADE SCHOOL
(1957 – 1958)
First Grade (Continued)

Student Enrollment	Parents
Donald Raymond Fleck	Martin and Paulette Flack
Jeri Ann Forsha	Bill and Marie Forsha
Dewey Izzard	Clark and Jean Izzard
Hilda Sue Mankin	Charles & Christie Mankin
Richard Derek Moore	Derek Scott and Flora Smith
Elizabeth Josephine Percifield	Ralph and Patsy Percifield
Ace Allan Redman	Worth and Lenora Redman
Peter Alexander Romanjenko	Ivan and Katherine Romanjenko
Edward Leon Sack	Bill and Irene Sack
Sandra Kay Sandy	George and Mary Sandy
Linda Gayle Study	Brooks and Cathryn Study
Timothy Stephen Tarver	Stephen & Ruth Tarver
Stephen Thomas Throne	Earl & Ethel Throne
Janie Rae Tyrrell	Lee, Jr and Audrey Tyrrell
Laura Ruth West	Leland and Jenny West

GILLETTE GRADE SCHOOL
(1958 – 1959)
First Grade
Salary: $4,500.00

Student Enrollment

Donna Renee Addison
Roger Kelly Brown
Stanley Elwood Cadotte
Ronald Roy Carlson
Gilbert Ray Cook
John Cullip
Jerry Dozier
Paul Andrew Drovdal
Curtis Lee Fleck
James Russell Garvey, Jr
Gary Gene Gleason
Connie Ray Houx
Jerelyn Jean Howard
Stanley George Hunter

Gloria Marie Lara
Linda Sue Luster
Rena Kay Marsh
Jesse Hugh McLaughlin
Deborah Sue Miller
Barbara Jane Morgan
James Walter O'Clair
Arline DeWitt Phillips
Beverly Jean Record
David Lee Reeder
Richard Leroy Shaffer
Linda Lee Thornton
Rae Ann Todd
Teri Lynn Varner
Hazel Alberta Wintermute

GILLETTE GRADE SCHOOL
(1959 – 1960)
First Grade
Salary: $4,740.00

Student Enrollment

Sherryl Louise Addison
Diana Gail Allen
Robin Lee Anderson
Janice Elaine Barlow
Karen Kay Bates
Roberta Kay Clements
Connie Ann Conrad
John Hasley Darnall
Deborah Kay Doud
Ronnie Garman
Cynthia Gray
Barbara Dee Hostetter
Jerald Duane Joslyn
Gene Lyle Hanson
Tommy Howard
Lonny Dee Lee
Charles Allen Light
Jani Lynch

Connie Sue McCormack
Donna Lucille McMahon
Patricia Jane McMillan
Darrell Martin Olds
Steven M. Osmo
Jimmy Alfred Percifield
Richard Brian Reeder
David William Rice
Carol Ann Saathoff
Sidney Dean Sidey
Glenda Kay Smelser
Margorie May Sparks
Linda Marie Stickney
Karen Elizabeth Tarver
Susan Martha Tholson
David Joe Vigil
Patricia Lynn Wolff

GILLETTE GRADE SCHOOL
(1960 – 1961)
First Grade
Salary: $4,860.00

Student Enrollment

Joseph Anthony Ballard
Linda Lee Beck
Richard Ernest Brannan
Katherine Ann Clark
Debra Lyn Clements
Linda Diane Coker
Bradley Coltrane
Patricia Cummings
Randy Bee Davis
Rhonda Eyre
Terry Wayne Rogers
Daneen Joy Ferguson
Thomas Bradford Field
Barbara Jean Freese
Douglas   Fitch
Lolynn Gerlach
Barbara Jo Graham
Renee Janice Green
Carol Gunter
Debra Harned
Linda Ann Hinsvark
Dianne Hollingsworth
MaRene Job
Kenneth Lane
Dennis Maier

McKinley Linn Morrison
Donelle Jean Marquiss
LaRon Dean Neugebauer,
Carmen Lee Norfolk
Zelda J. Odon
Bobby Pollok
Randy Darrell Prazma
Roy Kendal Renfro
Glada Michelle Roberts
Fred Romanjenko
Jimmy Shenk
Cheri Sheppard
David Dean Smith
Robert Smith
Ricky Sylvester
Susan Lynn Tholson
Myra Junann Toll
Deborah Waldrup
Robin Gay Whitham
Dianna Wilkenson

GILLETTE GRADE SCHOOL
(1961 – 1962)
First Grade
Salary: $5,160.00

Student	Father/Mother	Occupation
Dawne Ree Anderson	John and Betty Lou Anderson	Culligans
Melvin Belferstone		
Toby Lynn Bennick	J. L. and Ruth Bennick	
Mike Carry Blackley	J. C. and Joyce Blackley	District Manager
Rhonda Brannan	Wayne and Betty Lou Brannan	pumper
Stan Lee Carstens	Larry and Marvel Carstens	game warden
Charles William Davis		
Robert Phillip Doyle	Jack and Virginia Doyle	Engr Soil Cons. Service
Linda Jeanne Drovdal	Norris and Norma Drovdal	salesman
Loralei Forrest	Bob and Lois Forrest	oil field work
Melvin Lee Frasier	Melvin and Lucille Frasier	oil trucker
Sue Ellen Gulley	Donald and Dorothy Gulley	restaurant
Vicki Louise Harmon	Lloyd Harmon	driller
David Bruce Harrod	Ralph and Loa Jean Harrod	Highway Dept
Kelsey Hastings	John and Lydia Hastings	oil field work
Joyce Heimann	John and Iola Heimann	L & L (store)
Jody Marie Hughes	Woodie and Ethel Hughes	
Sharon Elaine Johnson	William and Joan Johnson	Wyodak Mine
Shirley Ann Joslyn	J. V. *Pete* and LaVonne Joslyn	Auto Body Shop

GILLETTE GRADE SCHOOL
(1961 – 1962)
First Grade (Continued)

Student	Father/Mother	Occupation
Norma Jean Kenitzer	Norman and Deloris Kenitzer	postal clerk
Kenneth Lane	Robert and Dorothy Showalter	nurse
Nancy Lou Mankin	Charles and Christie Mankin	insurance
Rose Renee Mapel	Roy and Rosemary Mapel	KIML Radio Station
Vicki Sue Marrington	Dean and Avis Marrington	plumber
Carla Joan Miller	Clifford and Darlene Miller	pipeline construction
Patricia Ann Morgan	James and Jean Morgan	Wyodak Resources
Jacqueline Moses	Milliard and Phyllis Moses	operator engineer
Gaylen Keith Neugebauer	Ronald and Marian Neugebauer	roughneck
Russell Lee Olds	Charlie and Vera Olds	insurance
Effie May Owen	Frank & Beatrice Owen	truck driver
Rayne Deane Phillips	Raymond and Junea Phillips	State Highway
Wanda Jean Robb		
Vicki Lynn Shipley	Harold and Belle Shipley	house mover
Mark Stegelman	Alfred and Lorian Stegleman	school teacher
Marla Stumpf	Gene and Shirley Stumpf	Mgr, Oil Well Supply
Timmy Clarence Thompson,	Robert and Edith Thompson	shop foreman
Tommy Curtis Thompson,	Robert and Edith Thompson	Shop Foreman
Marilyn Sue Unruh	Larry and Ercell Unruh	Coulter's
Harold Lee Worman	Truman and Patricia Worman	Farmer's Coop
David Wright	Billy Bob and Delores Wright	truck driver

GILLETTE GRADE SCHOOL
(1962-1963)
First Grade
Salary: $5,580.00

Student	Father/Mother	Occupation
Robert Earl Baity, Jr	Robert and Barbara Baity	barber
Jack Howard Banks	James (?) and Joyce Banks	engineer
Michael Francis Beck	Jerry and Iva Kay Beck	county
Richard Allen Bengston	Walter and Esther Bengston	painter
Debora Jean Bridwell	Robert and Charlotte Bridwell	Petrolane Co
Chris Everett Carroll	Floyd and Reba Carroll	mud engineer
Sharon Denise Coker	Emma Coker	waitress
Pamela Collins	Horace and Onita Collins	roughneck
Patrick David	Jackie and Patricia Cooper	tank setter
Lynne Coulson	Ruth Coulson (grandmother)	
George Henry Croisant	Eilene Croisant	
Gregory George Dallen	George and Joyce Dallen	seismograph
William Alfred Dendy	Daniel and Margaret Dendy	truck driver
Cindy Dent		
Donald Duncan		
Junetta Ruth Ettle	Dale and Beverly Ettle	service station manager
Rita Jean Flamm	Donald and Meda Flamm	Supervisor
James Herman Frick	James and Dorothy Frick	mechanic
Thomas Jefferson Gates	Frank and Bette Mathisen	carpenter
Bill Harmon	Don and Kyung Harmon	Oil Tank
Gary Lee Harper	William J. and Maxine Harper	tool pusher
Robert George Herrick	_____ and Janis Herrick	mine worker
Nancy Jean Hoven	Robert and Gladys Hoven	petrol operator
Sharon Jean Husted	Bobby and Jean Husted	mechanic
Rhonda Lynne Joslyn	Richard and Iris Joslyn	service station

GILLETTE GRADE SCHOOL
(1962-1963)
First Grade (Continued)

Student	Father/Mother	Occupation
Mark Evan Kinzer	Dick and Darlene Kinzer	coach
Peggy Ann MacEntire	Leslie and Ruth MacEntire	roughneck
Laura Ann May	Roy and Betty May	Gene's Furniture
Joenna Eve Nicolen	Jeanella Rae Nicolen	
Toya Olsen		
Gregory Pickett		
Michael E. Randolph		
H. Paul Schiess		
Larry Kirk Smith	Jerry and Barbara Smith	electronics tech
Robert Strand		
Dixie J. Wiedrick		

GILLETTE GRADE SCHOOL
(1963 – 1964)
First Grade
Salary: $5,580.00

(No class enrollment or photo available)

GILLETTE GRADE SCHOOL
(1964 – 1965)
First Grade
Salary: $6,204.00

Student	Father/Mother	Occupation
Steven John Beck	Jerry and Iva Beck	County
Martha Jane Bradford	Johnny and Clara Bradford	Seismograph
Rayburn Lee Bradford	Johnny and Clara Bradford	Seismograph
Douglas Earl Briggs	Robert and Sandra Douglas	Telephone Office
Peggy Sue Bingham	Homer Bingham	Service Engineer
Christina Brunson	David Brunson	oil field worker
Terry Don Campbell	Jerry Campbell	Mechanic
Bill Andrew Carson		
William Daniel Cochran	William Cochran	plumber
Michael Dwaine Cooper	Manuel and Virginia Cooper	Delta Drilling Co
Cynthia Lee Coulson	B. J. and Ruth Coulson	Retired
Susan Faye Cummings	Harold and Irene Cummings	pumper
Mary Alice Davila	John Davila	driller
Margaret Irene Drovdal	Norris and Norma Drovdal	salesman
Gerald Dwaine Frick	James and Dorothy Frick	mechanic
Rebecca Jane Gulley	Donald and Dorothy Gulley	Sands Hotel
Linda Anne Harrod	LaVern and Lillian Harrod	school custodian
Lillian Marie Isbell	William and Sandy Isbell	operating engineer
Lorie Lynn Kinzer	Richard and Darleen Kinzer	teacher/coach
Jacob Christian Koenig	David and Katherine Koenig	truck driver
William Robert Kurht	Albert and Beverly Kurht	truck driver
Thomas Jay LaOrange	George and Kathryn LaOrange	store manager
Janet Lee McClelland	John and Mary Ruth	car salesman
Connie May Mattke	Leroy Mattke	
Connie Sue Miller	Dorse and Rose Miller	radio announcer
Michael Glen Tholson	Glen Tholson	telephone co
Kathlene Ann Webb	Fred Webb	mechanic
Sandra Lee Weber	Clarence Weber	telephone co
Diana Lynn Wolff	Vincent Wolff	rancher

CENTRAL ELEMENTARY SCHOOL
(FORMERLY GILLETTE GRADE SCHOOL)
(1965 – 1966)
First Grade
Salary: $6,722.00

CENTRAL - GRADE 1 - ROOM 1 H

Student Enrollment

Travis Lee Adsit

Peggy Sue Ballard

James Allen Bing

Frederick Lee Borne

Cindy Leann Campbell

Jacklyn Ann Comer

Marvin Ennis Franklin

Donnie Ray Gardner

Kay Lorene Gulley

Owen Henry Hovland

Virgil Jeffery

Robert Wayne Kron

Julie Claire McIntosh

Linda Ruth Meserve

Karen Ann Miller

David Allen Mondle

Janice Lee Morrow

Jeffrey John Sherman

Teresa Louise Sindelar

Ivan Lee Snell

Jackie Bruce Spelts

Lloyd Kent Thomason

Kathy Lynn Unruh

Lisa Annette Waller

Brenda Sue Willoughby

Calvin Lloyd Winland

Karen Christine Worman

Susan Lea Wright

Geraldine Raye Zahn

WESTSIDE ELEMENTARY SCHOOL
(1966 – Spring 1975)

West 6th Street
Gillette, Campbell County, Wyoming

WESTSIDE ELEMENTARY SCHOOL
GILLETTE, WYOMING
First Grade
(1966 – 1967)
Salary: $6,800.00

(List of students missing; no class photo)

WESTSIDE ELEMENTARY SCHOOL
GILLETTE, WYOMING
(1967 – 1968)
First Grade
Salary: $7,000.00

(No class photo available)

Student	Father/Mother	Occupation
Ricky Dee Baker	Lawrence and Sherry Baker	oil field
John Eugene Baley	Ralph and Bertha Baley	oil field
Paul Wayne Beckley	Paul and Arvella Beckley	driller
Amber Gay Bellamy	Kurt and Gloria Belamy	oil field
John Leslie Crump	John and Doris Crump	service station
James Martin Dunbar	Joseph and Janice Dunbar	self-employed
Paul Edward Gates	George and Cecelia Gates	custodian
Thomas Acquinas Haller	James and Irene Haller	
William Walter Harrod	Ralph and Jean Harrod	highway dept
Lorinda Ann Howard	Adolph and Jocelyn Harrod	Winland Diary
Buddy Leroy Huseth	Vernon and Carolyn Huseth	driller
Tammy Joan Kottraba	James and Edith Kottraba	mechanic; telephone operator
Brian Kelley McCormack	James and Marjorie McCormack	machine operator
Robert Dale Schmidt	Dale (dec'd) and Donna Schmidt	housewife
Randall Jay Sober	Jerry and Doris Sober	driller
Marvin Lee Summers	Kenneth & Julia Summers	roustabout
David Neal Swingle	Leonard and Norma Jean Swingle	teacher
Timothy James Wenger	Sammy and Terry Wenger	mechanic

WESTSIDE ELEMENTARY SCHOOL
GILLETTE, WYOMING
(1968 – 1969)
First Grade
Salary: $7,500.00

(Note: Gary Allen Whisler middle of second row; grandson of Ton and Mildred Whisler)

WESTSIDE ELEMENTARY SCHOOL
GILLETTE, WYOMING
(1968 – 1969)
First Grade (continued)

Partial List of Children:

James Cody
Yvonne Collom
Tamara Defoe
Judy Hawley
Cheri Joyce
Luena Lest
Craig Miller
Robert Momders
Robert Powell
Darleen Stanton
Kimberlee Stokes
Gary Allen Whisler
Yvonne Whitham

(Note: Names of children taken from the back of their pictures given to their teacher; all other pictures not identified)

Partial List of Children:

Melanie_____
Chipper _____
Keith _____
Scott Barber
Cherlyn Chitwood
John Crump
Mary Edelman
Becky Franzen
Wayne Franzen
Jill Glover
Brett Graham
Bruce Kenitzer
Mark Kuntz
Tracy McFarley
Christine Newton
Debbie Stephens
Debbie Wallace
Vikki Werger

(Note: Names of children taken from the back of their pictures given to their teacher; all other pictures not identified)

WESTSIDE ELEMENTARY SCHOOL
GILLETTE, WYOMING
(1970 – 1971)
First Grade
Salary: $12,137.00

(No class photo available)

Student	Father/Mother	Occupation
Condida Betts	(Deceased) and Sharon Betts	bank teller
Jeri Lynne Clements	Lester and Sharon Clements	Gillette-O-Matic
Jerry Sue Cundiff	Jerry and Sue Cundiff	welder
Tammy Decker	Gary and Lynda Decker	store manager
Tarla Gates	George and Cecelia Gates	custodian
Kevin Harnett	Lawrence and Sharon Harnett	field engineer
Lisa Ann Haug	Conrad and Ruth Ann Haug	salesman
Tellison James Hertzog	Paul and Rosemary Hertzog	water hauler
Karen Hladky	D. B. *Spike* and Margaret Ann Hladky	sheriff
Joseph Hubbard	John and Irene Hubbard	bodyman
Daniel Kingsley	Freeman and Sandy Mark	police officer
Stephan Kremers	Ed and Theresa Kremers	tool pusher
Robin Kuntz	Lawrence and Pat Kuntz	tool pusher
Darren Lynde	Darryl and Sharon Lynde	teacher
Barbara Marez	Alfred and Patricia Marez	unit operator
John Nash	Harriet Nash	teacher
Lisa Ann Rhode	William and Alice Rhode	heavy equipment
Brandy Rubis	Dell and Alice Rubis	warehouseman
Dalene Ruby	Jesse and Margorie Ruby	well driller
Jon Patrick Smith	Delbert and June Smith	cementer
Mark Sorheim	Clare and Suzanne Sorheim	highway dept
Linda Sprigler	Leo and Iola Sprigler	mechanic
James Young	Butch and Sherry Young	truck driver

Miss Leona S. Heptner

WESTSIDE ELEMENTARY SCHOOL
GILLETTE, WYOMING
(1971 – 1972)
First Grade
Salary: $12,830.00

(List of students missing; no class photo)

WESTSIDE ELEMENTARY SCHOOL
GILLETTE, WYOMING
(1972 – 1973)
First Grade
Salary: $12,830.00

(No class photo available)

Student	Father/Mother	Occupation
Traci Albers		
Kevin Carson	Joseph and Darleen Carson	
James Casady	Roy and Claudette Casady	
Kelly Craig	Darrel and Sina Craig	
Robert Dolcater	Robert and Betty Dolcater	
Catherine Edleman	Anthony and Patricia Edleman	
Anthony Fish	M. Lee and Janice Fish	
Carl Gossett	Frances and Emma Lou Gossett	
Mark Green	M. L. and Jeanette Green	
Robert Heald	Robert and Jessie Heald	
Gary Knigge	Gordon and Mary Knigge	
Gary Knotts	Marshall and Patty Knotts	
Troy Lajeunesse	George and Betty Lajeunesse	
Sherianne Martin		
Jamie McCawley	Dale and Susan McCawley	
Deanne Meyer	Harlan and Lily Meyer	
Tommy Oliver	Thomas Oliver	
Alicia Patterson	Karen Patterson	
Weslie Roulter	James and Linda Roulter	
David Rossie	Raymond and Judy Rossie	
Peggy Ruth Scott	Donald and Ruth Scott	
Duane Stroup	Ned and Glenda Stroup	
Rhonda Marie Tarno	Melvin and Elsie Tarno	
Sheila Underwood	Russell and Donna Underwood	
Kendia Williams	Robert and Charlotte Williams	

WESTSIDE ELEMENTARY SCHOOL
GILLETTE, WYOMING
(1973 – 1974)
Second Grade
Salary: $13,005.00

232

WESTSIDE ELEMENTARY SCHOOL
GILLETTE, WYOMING
(1973-1974)
Second Grade (continued)

Partial List of Children:

Julie Callender
Alan Curl
David Divis
Michael Engler
Ronnie Griffith
Evelyn Hartshorn
Noreane Helms
Tammy Hladky
Penny Johnson
Duane Joslyn
Chris Knapp
Sheri Leiker
Paul Lukehart
Oundalyn Malone
Suzy Medlock
Tammy Nuzum
Doris Plato
Robbie Renning
Kirby Roberts
Lanita Scott
Lance Shea
Jeff Slattery
Julie Smith
Derran Sucher
Tyrus Rus Taylor
Tammy Warner

(Note: Names of children taken from the back of their pictures given to their teacher; all other pictures not identified)

WESTSIDE ELEMENTARY SCHOOL
GILLETTE, WYOMING
(1974 – 1975)
Second Grade

Salary: $14,385.00

(List of students missing; no class photo)

Leona retired from teaching at the end of this school term

Miss Heptner

Jeanette Heptner and Allyson Sicks
(About 1980)

JEANETTE LOUISE HEPTNER
(Teaching Years 1941 – 1977)

Jeanette began her first year of teaching at the Upper Cabin Creek School in Crook County near Oshoto. She had first been assigned a $50.00 a month school near Recluse which began on August 29, 1941. However, this position only lasted until September 8th. She was offered, and she accepted, a teaching position at the Upper Cabin Creek School. Her mother and brother Eugene came after her at Recluse and took her to the Charles Haubers on September 9, 1941, to meet with the school board. Jeanette boarded with the Charles Holbin family while teaching the 1941-1942 term at the Upper Creek School.

After teaching the 1947-1948 junior high class at Rozet Consolidated School, Rozet, Wyoming, Jeanette decided to quit teaching and go to college full time. That fall she enrolled at the University of Wyoming at Laramie. She went year-round. In the summer of 1950, Leona joined her during the summer semester. During the last year at the University, Jeanette stayed with Mrs. Henry Taylor. Jeanette graduated from the University of Wyoming, College of Education, with a Bachelor of Arts Degree on June 4, 1951. That fall she received an Elementary Life Certificate from the State of Wyoming Department of Education. This certificate entitled her to teach in high schools, elementary schools and rural schools in the state of Wyoming for life.

The fall of September 1951 Jeanette began teaching the second-grade class in the Cowley Elementary School, Cowley, Wyoming. She taught there three school terms. At that time, she believed that a teacher should only teach for three years in one school, so in 1954, she accepted a position teaching second grade in the Gertrude Burns Elementary School, Newcastle, Weston County, Wyoming. She taught there for 23 years from September 1954 until her retirement in June 1977.

The summer before Jeanette started teaching at Newcastle she began her studies towards a Master's Degree in Education. She attended summer semesters for seven years at the Nebraska State Teachers College, Chadron, Nebraska. As a project she needed towards obtaining her Master's Degree, Jeanette organized the first Parent-Teacher Association (PTA) Conferences for the Gertrude Burns School. On July 28, 1960, Jeanette received her Degree of Master of Science in Education from the Nebraska State Teachers College, at Chadron, Nebraska.

Between September 1960 and June 1970, Jeanette supervised, in her classroom at Gertrude Burns Elementary, ten student teachers from the University of Wyoming, College of Education. On May 21, 1974 Jeanette was awarded a Certificate of Appreciation from the University of Wyoming in recognition of her ten years of participation in the University's student teaching program. The ten student teachers Jeanette guided through the mechanics and rewards of teaching children were:

Diane Markley	1960 – 1961
Jean Smith	1961 – 1962
Janet Lynn	1962 – 1963
Louise Trowe	1963 - 1964
Marilyn Rahmig	1964 – 1965
Linda Porter	1965 – 1966
Carol Cook	1966 – 1967
Wanda Drake	1967 – 1968
Jeanne Love	1968 – 1969
Sue Riggs	1969 – 1970

At the age of 57 Jeanette resigned from the Gertrude Burns Elementary School on June 29, 1977, after thirty-five years of teaching - the past twenty-three years at Gertrude Burns. Upon her retirement, she moved back to Gillette to live with her sister, Leona, at 412 Circle Drive.

Jeanette pursued other interests outside her classroom:

She had been a member of the First Presbyterian Church, Gillette, Wyoming, since 1947. After moving back to Gillette upon her retirement from teaching, Jeanette, with the help of her sister Leona, organized the Emergency Closet (TEC Shop). The closet was a special project sponsored by the First Presbyterian Church. The TEC Shop accepted donations of used clothing and household essentials for helping low income people in emergency situations. Jeanette served as a Deacon in 1984-1985.

She joined the Theta Chapter of Delta Kappa Gamma Society, Gillette, Wyoming, on November 8, 1958. During the time Jeanette spent in Newcastle Jeanette helped to organize a new charter chapter of Delta Kappa Gamma Society International. Effective March 17, 1962, she transferred from the Theta Chapter at Gillette, Wyoming, to the new Lambda Chapter, Delta Kappa Gamma Society International, at Newcastle, Wyoming, as a charter member. She served as its first President. After her retirement from teaching, she transferred in December 1977 to the Theta Chapter, Delta Kappa Gamma, in Gillette. On May 11, 1978, the Lamda Chapter of Delta Kappa Gamma at Newcastle chose to name their high school scholarship the *Jeanette Heptner Recruitment Grant*.

Jeanette joined the Pythian Sisters of Pythagoras Temple No. 8, Newcastle, Wyoming. She served as the secretary from January 5, 1962, to January 5, 1965. Jeanette completed her term of most Excellent Chief of Pythian Temple No. 8, on December 31, 1974, and was then entitled to receive the rank of Past Chief and become a member of the Grand Temple of Wyoming. In 1976, she was elected to be a representative to the Grand Temple of the Order of Pythian Sisters.

On March 13, 1967, Jeanette joined Gateway Rebekah Lodge No. 37, Newcastle, Wyoming. She was elected as their Noble Grand in 1971. She served as District Deputy President 1972-1973. On December 21, 1978, Jeanette transferred from the Gateway Rebekah Lodge No. 37 in Newcastle to the Jewel Rebekah Lodge No. 28 in Gillette, Wyoming. She served as Noble Grand for Jewel Rebekah Lodge No. 28 in 1982 and again in 1996. On November 13, 1988, the Jewel Rebekah Lodge honored Jeanette and Leona with the Decoration of Chivalry, the highest honor given by the Lodge. Jeanette served as the District Deputy President for Jewel Rebekah Lodge No. 28 in 1998-1999.

Jeanette's hobbies included traveling, oil and pastel painting, pencil drawing, knitting, crocheting, sewing, and teaching her young Cooper great-grandnephews how to play cards from Old Maid to cribbage to seven-up. In the 1990s, she bought herself a personal computer and then commenced to teach herself how to operate it, with the aid of her great-grandnephew, Dustin Cooper. Along with using it for personal correspondence and committee notes, she became quite the expert at exchanging email notes with her nieces in Virginia, her grandnephews in California and Arizona, and with other friends and acquaintances.

JEANETTE'S TEACHING ASSIGNMENTS

TERMS	NAME	WHERE
1941 – 1942	Upper Cabin Creek School	Oshoto, Crook County, WY
1942 – 1943	Poison Creek School	Hulett, Crook County, WY
1943 – 1944	Whisler School	Rozet, Campbell County, WY
1944 – 1945	Whisler School	Rozet, Campbell County, WY
1945 – 1946	Whisler School	Rozet, Campbell County, WY
1946 – 1947	Kintz-Mills School	Lawver, Campbell County, WY
1947 – 1948	Rozet Consolidated School	Rozet, Campbell County, WY
1948 – 1951	(Student at the University of Wyoming, College of Education, Laramie, Wyoming)	
1951 – 1952	Cowley Elementary School	Cowley, Big Horn County, WY
1952 – 1953	Cowley Elementary School	Cowley, Big Horn County, WY
1953 – 1954	Cowley Elementary School	Cowley, Big Horn County, WY
1954 – 1955	Gertrude Burns Elementary	Newcastle, Weston County, WY
1955 – 1956	Gertrude Burns Elementary	Newcastle, Weston County, WY
1956 – 1957	Gertrude Burns Elementary	Newcastle County, Weston, WY
1957 – 1958	Gertrude Burns Elementary	Newcastle, Weston County, WY
1958 – 1959	Gertrude Burns Elementary	Newcastle, Weston County, WY
1959 – 1960	Gertrude Burns Elementary	Newcastle, Weston County, WY
1960 – 1961	Gertrude Burns Elementary	Newcastle, Weston County, WY
1961 – 1962	Gertrude Burns Elementary	Newcastle, Weston County, WY
1962 1963	Gertrude Burns Elementary	Newcastle, Weston County, WY
1963 – 1964	Gertrude Burns Elementary	Newcastle, Weston County, WY
1964 – 1965	Gertrude Burns Elementary	Newcastle, Weston County, WY
1965 – 1966	Gertrude Burns Elementary	Newcastle, Weston County, WY
1966 – 1967	Gertrude Burns Elementary	Newcastle, Weston County, WY
1967 – 1968	Gertrude Burns Elementary	Newcastle, Weston County, WY
1968 – 1969	Gertrude Burns Elementary	Newcastle, Weston County, WY
1969 – 1970	Gertrude Burns Elementary	Newcastle, Weston County, WY
1970 – 1971	Gertrude Burns Elementary	Newcastle, Weston County, WY
1971 – 1972	Gertrude Burns Elementary	Newcastle, Weston County, WY
1972 – 1973	Gertrude Burns Elementary	Newcastle, Weston County, WY
1973 – 1974	Gertrude Burns Elementary	Newcastle, Weston County, WY
1974 – 1975	Gertrude Burns Elementary	Newcastle, Weston County, WY
1975 – 1976	Gertrude Burns Elementary	Newcastle, Weston County, WY
1976 – 1977	Gertrude Burns Elementary	Newcastle, Weston County, WY
1977 -	RESIGNED FROM TEACHING	

UPPER CABIN CREEK SCHOOL
Oshoto, Crook County, Wyoming
(1941 – 1942)

Students:	Shirley Reynolds	Elvin Rush
	David Reynolds	Sylvia Rush
	Wayne Reynolds	Lyle Hill

This school was located in the vicinity of the Devil's Tower National Monument, the first national monument to be created by Congress on September 24, 1906. During this term *Devil's Tower George* parachuted down to the top of the Devil's Tower. At night, the children could see the flood light that was lowered onto the top of the tower until a team of expert climbers arrived to help *Devil's Tower George* climb down from the top of the Tower.

Jeanette boarded with Mr. and Mrs. Charles Holbin that winter. She paid thirty dollars for her room and board. That left twenty dollars of her paycheck to do other things with. The school was in rough country. However, when they had their Christmas School Program everyone in the community came. Even Leona and Eugene drove over from Rozet to attend.

POISON CREEK SCHOOL
HULETT, CROOK COUNTY, WYOMING
(1942 – 1943)

Students:	Bill Glover	Anna Atkinson
	Joyce Glover	Albert Atkinson
	Russell Gray	Lionel Atkinson

The three Atkinson children moved away during the school year, leaving the remaining three to finish out the school term without them. Jeanette roomed and boarded with Mrs. Glover. The school joined with Nelle Wennade's school for an end-of-the-school-year picnic. Leona and Eugene also attended.

Jeanette Heptner
(At Poison Creek School, 1942–1943)

WHISLER SCHOOL
ROZET, CAMPBELL COUNTY, WYOMING
(1943 – 1944)

Students: Lorna Whisler   Delores Whisler
              Donnie Whisler

It was located about one and one-half miles west of Laura Heptner's farm which placed it about halfway between there and Slim and Irene Whisler's farm. David and Marge Whisler, the parents of Donnie and Delores, had moved across the road east of the Heptners, on the former Charlie Woods homestead. The school was a mobile-type school; it was brought in on a truck bed and placed on a rough foundation built by Slim Whisler. Just south of the schoolhouse, outside of the fenced-in school yard (from cattle) there was a sandstone canyon that had been blown out by wind and shaped by many thunderstorms. This was the children's favorite place to play during noon recess when they weren't playing sagebrush baseball.

WHISLER SCHOOL
ROZET, CAMPBELL COUNTY, WYOMING
(1944-1945)

Students: Lorna Whisler   Delores Whisler
                     Donnie Whisler   Barbara Whisler

This was the Christmas that the teacher, Jeanette Heptner, almost burned the school building down during the Christmas Program. The Christmas tree, a cedar, caught on fire. The tree was decorated with wax candles placed in candleholders that were clipped to the tree branches. The candles were lighted for everyone to enjoy during the school's Christmas program. Before the evening was over the teacher noticed the tree was beginning to burn. She could pinch the flames out, but not until the ceiling of the school building was scorched a bit—a reminder of what could have happened. This was the last year Jeanette used her wax candles and holders.

While Jeanette was teaching at the Gertrude Burns School in Newcastle, Wyoming, the people managing the Anna Miller Museum wanted decorations for an old-fashioned Christmas tree they were putting up in the museum. Jeanette donated her wax candles and their holders to them. They were numbered and placed in their collection with the above story and may be found on display at the Anna Miller Museum in Newcastle, Wyoming.

WHISLER SCHOOL
ROZET, CAMPBELL COUNTY, WYOMING
(1945 – 1946)

Students:
> Back Row: Lorna Whisler, Donnie Whisler, Delores Whisler,
> and Miss Heptner
> Front Row: Olive Whisler (occasionally) and Barbara Whisler

Lorna's mother sent her sister Olive to school with her on days when the weather was good. She soon became a once-a-week kindergarten student. The children continued to play down in the sandstone canyon, mostly cowboys and Indians. It was their favorite place for Easter egg hunts. They also played sagebrush softball outside the school fence and other typical games inside the schoolyard, such as Annie Over, Fox and Geese (in the winter time), Pick-up-Sticks, Red Rover, etc.

School Picnic, Spring 1946
Adults: Grandma Heptner, Marge Whisler, Slim Whisler, Irene Whisler, David Whisler
Kids: Delores Whisler, Donnie Whisler, Olive Whisler, Lorna Whisler, and Barbara Whisler

KINTZ-MILLS SCHOOL
LAWVER, CAMPBELL COUNTY, WYOMING
(1946 – 1947)

Students:	Reynard Mills	Merna Jo Kintz
	Clarabelle Mills	Jim Kintz
	Raleigh Mills	

From Jeanette's notes: "This school was located about thirty miles southeast of Gillette. Jim Kintz was always comparing the size of things. Listening to him talk one day, his teacher, Jeanette Heptner, realized he thought the smoke stacks at the Wyodak Coal Mine were much smaller than they were. The teacher explained to him that they were much larger than his mother's washtub and that they were even larger than his dad's stock watering tank. Jim couldn't believe it. But the next time his dad went to Wyodak to fetch some coal Jim rode along. The class didn't hear any more about the Wyodak smoke stacks and how small they were.

"Carroll *Slim* Whisler was learning to fly an airplane. One day he flew over the schoolhouse and waved his wings at the children on the ground. The kids did not know quite what to think about this flying event."

ROZET CONSOLIDATED SCHOOL
ROZET, CAMPBELL COUNTY, WYOMING
(1947 – 1948)

JUNIOR HIGH/SEVENTH AND EIGHTH GRADE CLASS

Students:
   Back Row: Norma Preston, Edna Thompson, Darrell Heptner, Arlene Bryant,
               Miss Heptner
   Front Row: John Baker, Emma Brunson, Shirley Heptner, Ruth Potter, Hugh Baker

(Note: Jeanette took the next four years off from teaching to attend the University of Wyoming, Laramie, Wyoming, working towards her Bachelor of Arts Degree in Education. She graduated on June 4, 1951. Then she began attending summer sessions at Nebraska State Teachers College, Chadron, Nebraska, working towards her Master of Science in Education Degree. Ten summers later she graduated on July 28, 1960.)

BACHELOR OF ARTS DEGREE IN EDUCATION
University of Wyoming, Laramie, Wyoming

June 4, 1951

MASTER OF SCIENCE DEGREE IN EDUCATION

Summer Commencement
Thursday, July 28, 1960
7:30 P.M.
Elliot Memorial Stadium
Nebraska State Teachers College
Chadron, Nebraska

246

COWLEY ELEMENTARY SCHOOL
COWLEY, BIG HORN COUNTY, WYOMING
(1951 – 1954)

Old Cowley Elementary School

Playground

COWLEY ELEMENTARY SCHOOL
COWLEY, BIG HORN COUNTY, WYOMING

Upon graduating from the University of Wyoming in June 1951 Jeanette accepted a position at the Cowley Elementary School, teaching second grade. She enjoyed teaching these children and remembers her first class there with a special fondness. She lived in the basement of the home of James Harston. It must be noted that the dress code of the time was that the girls always wore dresses, the boys wore Levis or bib overalls and always with a button up shirt.

(1951 – 1952)

SECOND GRADE CLASS (GIRLS)
Left to right: _____, Roseann Acton, Myra Welling, Annette Welch, _____, _____

SECOND GRADE CLASS (BOYS)
Left to right: _____, David Frost, John Lewis, Don Baird,
Bob Acton, Delbert Parker, Dean Blakely, _____

Standing: Carolyn Lewis, Helen Partridge, Mary Helen
    Stubbs, Mac Crosby, Bruce Cook, Frances Juarez,
    Sylvia Stubbs, Nick Monk, Mike Little, Bob Gelock,
    Tookie Brightly, Richard Wilson, Ned Snell, Jay ___
Kneeling: Dean Netherton, Don Eyre, George Welch,
    Jim Acton, Unknown, Sherman _____, Eileen
    Yorgason, Clara Gifford, Leslie Asay, Bobby Jo
    Welch, Sally George, Delia Blakely

Cowley Elementary School 1951-1952

First, Second, Third Grade Picnic in Monk's Apple Orchard
Fall 1951

One event Jeanette remembers during her three years' teaching at this school was a First, Second, and Third Grade picnic at Monk's Apple Orchard. The first thing one of the boys did was to pick up a baby owl that had fallen out of its nest to the ground under a tree. Jeanette took the bird very carefully from him so that its claws would not scratch the boy and put him back into its nest. With the bird safe, the kids went on their merry way. Another thing the kids wanted to do that day was to go touch the *Prayer Rock*. It was on the other side of a canal. The kids assured their teacher that they could walk across a tree trunk that had fallen across the canal. So off they all went including Miss Heptner to see the *Prayer Rock*.

The story of the *Prayer Rock* as told to Jeanette by her students was that some time ago the rock was in the way when the people wanted to build a canal through the town of Cowley. The town had no large equipment to move it. One day a group of people gathered, put their hands on the rock, and prayed. The rock began to move, and they were able to push it out of the way of the canal. From that day on, the rock was called the *Prayer Rock*.

249

COWLEY ELEMENTRY SCHOOL
COWLEY, BIG HORN COUNTY, WYOMING
(1952 – 1953)

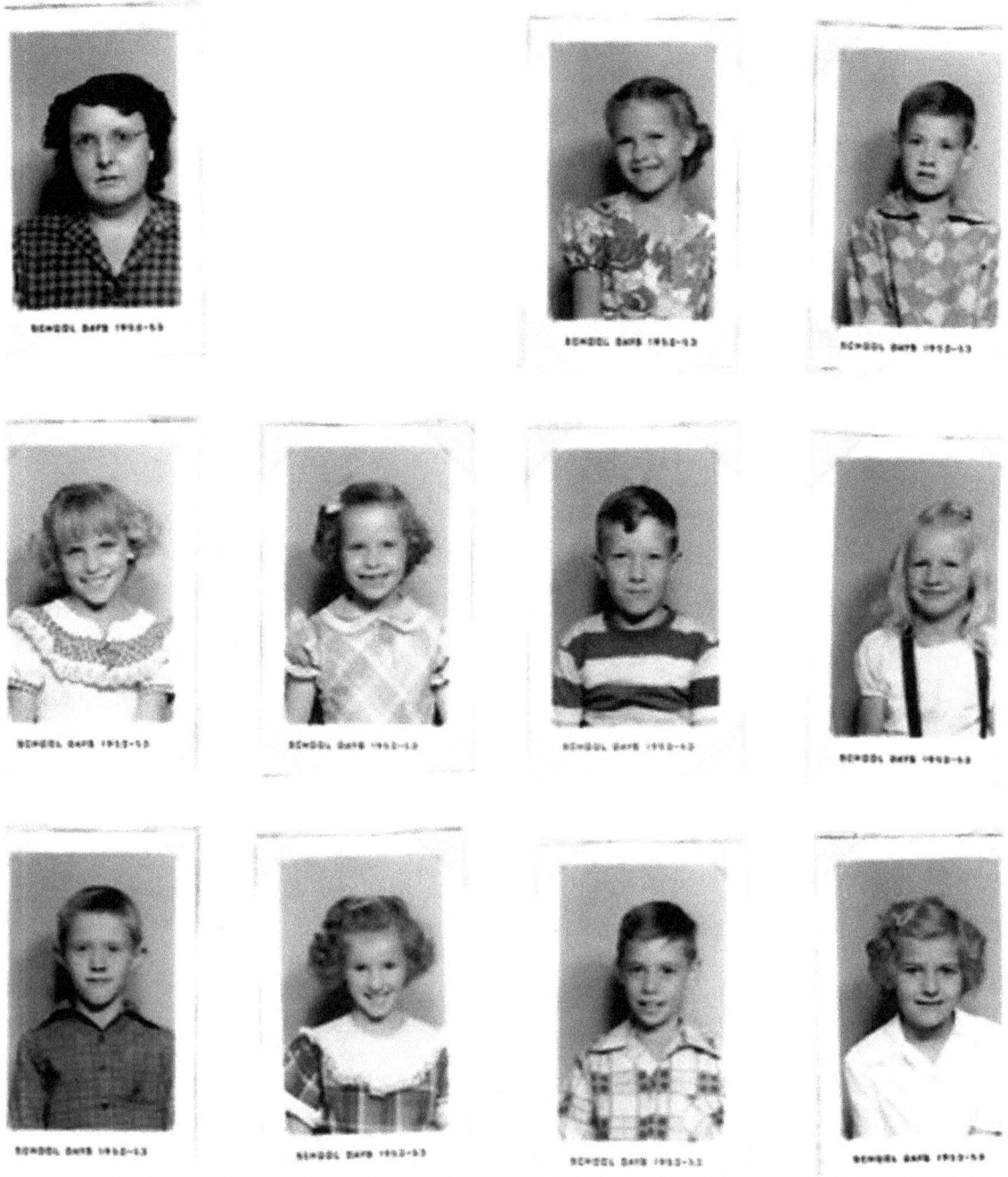

1st row: Miss Heptner, Lorraine Lewis, _____

2nd row: Barbara Monk, _____, Dick Lowery, Connie Parker

3rd row: Bill Harston, Christine Tebbs, Wade Welch, Peggy Marchant

COWLEY ELEMENTRY SCHOOL
(1952 – 1953) (Continued)

1st row: Grover Shaw, Wayne Holyoak, Edward Jensen, Annette Welch
2nd row: _____ (maybe Linda Asay), Jerry Partridge, Carolyn Crosby, Della Blakely
3rd row: Helen Partridge, Neil Simmons, John Snelders, Steven Cozzens

  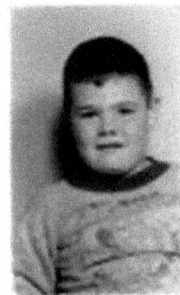 

1st row: Lorraine Lewis, Keith Rasmussen
2nd row: Tookie Brightly Shidler, Bobbie Jo Welch, Jim Acton, Linda Welling
3rd row: Ronnie Monk, Don Eyre, Linda Lou Blank, Darlene Banks

COWLEY ELEMENTARY SCHOOL
COWLEY, BIG HORN COUNTY, WYOMING
(1953 – 1954)

New Cowley Elementary School

(Jeanette did not list the names of these children on the back of the photo, only the year 1953-1954)

In the fall of 1953 the children and staff moved into a new Cowley Elementary School. Although Jeanette enjoyed Cowley this would be her last year at Cowley Elementary School because she believed, at that time, three years at one school was long enough, and she should make room for other teachers to come into the community and teach. She also wanted to get a little closer to her family on the eastern side of the Big Horn Mountains. Jeanette left with fond memories of the children and their families whom she got to know in Big Horn County.

GERTRUDE BURNS ELEMENTARY SCHOOL
NEWCASTLE, WESTON COUNTY, WYOMING

(September 1954 – June 1977)

    In the fall of 1954, Jeanette began teaching the second-grade class at the Gertrude Burns Elementary School. She remained there until her retirement from teaching in June 1977.

GERTRUDE BURNS ELEMENTARY SCHOOL
(1954 – 1955)

Students: 1st Row: Carole Wilson, Judith Statler, Beth Ann Cummings, Barbara Huber, Carolyn Rich, Beth Marie Johnson, Judy Bond, Debby Stephenson, Judy Snyder, Virginia Clere, Rhonda McCamley, Maryetta Begley, Sharon Kennedy

2nd Row: Eldon Wolfe, Jeffrey Sands, Randy Schmidt, Larry Nolder, Emily Gore, Vicki Matheny, Frank DeCastro, Jerry Snyder, Yoy Johnson, Gene Lawson, Larry Decker

3rd Row: Miss Heptner, Charles Fowler, Glenn Span, Jimmy Rodgers, Danny Montoya, Jerry Humes

GERTRUDE BURNS ELEMENTARY SCHOOL
(1955 – 1956)

Students: 1st Row: Shirley Rundell, Terry Lee Radcliffe, Judy Kay
                         Christensen, Kathleen Ann *Kath*y Allen, Agnes
                         *Kath*y Porter, Jacqueline *Jackie* Russell, Barbara
                         Hildebrand, Maxine Sachau, Nancy Margaret Wright
             2nd Row: Mary Ione Riley, Cynthia *Cindy* Orcutt, Eugene Earl
                         Martin, Donald Lee Galloway, Duane Nygard, Mike
                         Cummings, Larry Eugene Middagh, Ida May Poyner,
                         Sandra Kay Cullum
             3rd Row: Louis Anderson, Mark Chapson, William *Billy* Warren
                         Ford, Terry Russell Currey, Albert Kosderka, Lester
                         Clair Weir, Ivan *Butch* Metzler, Marvin Phoenix,
                         Larry Allen Lamb, Merwyn Steinberger

GERTRUDE BURNS ELEMENTARY SCHOOL
(1956 – 1957)

Students: 1st Row: Brenda Cromer, Linda Odland, Vickie Rich, Linda
                         Diane Johnson, Colleen Curtis, Nancy Oslund, Dixie
                         Davis, Anna Johnson, Marilyn Kock, Cathy Mills,
                         Sandra Rodgers
             2nd Row: Paul Mundschenk, Floyd Burdick, Judy Rundell, Dianne
                         Davis, Sandra East, Bonnie Tanner, Carl Johnson,
                         Jimmy McVay, Loren Ackley, Donald Jandreau
             3rd Row: Larry Archer, Norman Sedig, Danny Allen, Richard
                         Latham, Mike Hoff, Jimmy Fall, Jerry Lightman

GERTRUDE BURNS ELEMENTARY SCHOOL
(1957 – 1958)

GERTRUDE BURNS SCHOOL   2ND GRADE 1958   BUTLER STUDIO   Newcastle, Wyo.

Students: 1st Row: Debbie Kerns, Ruth Shook, Cecilia Gulley, Kathryn Tetrick, Clarice Jacobs, Elizabeth Colich, Judy Elliott, _____, Norma Lynn Cailler, Jackie Hartinger

                      2nd Row: Arthur Foster, Johnnie Steuble, Edith Shell, _____, Joella Pshara, _____, _____, Louise Brown, Willis Anderson, Tommy Fulton

                      3rd Row: Gregory Taylor, _____, Larry Erickson, Dale Underhill, Freddie Pate, _____, Mark Thompson, David Dybwad, Randy Ross, Paul McKay, _____

(Not pictured: Janis Mindschenk)

GERTRUDE BURNS ELEMENTARY SCHOOL
(1958 – 1959)

Students: 1st Row: Diane Ross, Connie Eisenbarth, Kay Hayman, Romona East, Elaine Oyler, Peggy Duclo, Cindy Fitzpatrick, Rhonda Henderson, Patty Farnsworth

                    2nd Row: Stephen Archer, Vallen Walker, Gary Gulley, Kathy Morgan, Pam Hoff, Arlene Wocicki, Vicki Darnall, Gary Wolfe, Melvin Poppleton, Mike Reber

                    3rd Row: Tommy Slocum, Mike Bartsch, Mark Berdahl, Jack Roan, Rodney Stensrud, Pat Allen, Charles Pzinski, Jack Loebs

(Not pictured: Arlyce Hieb)

GERTRUDE BURNS ELEMENTARY SCHOOL
(1959 – 1960)

Students: 1st Row: Lee Ray Denny, Kris Rowles, Jeffrey Silbaugh, Rodney
                         Smith, Harry Devereaux
             2nd Row: Laura Wegher, Colleen Caillier, Sharon Martens,
                         Kristine Johanson, Roxanne McCoy, Kristine Watson,
                         Scherry Litherland, Pamela McColley, Sherry Johnson
             3rd Row: Sammy Wade, Miss Heptner, Brent Sundstrom, Bryan
                         Sheehan, Bobby Scissions, Steven Preston, Thomas
                         Young, Jack Shook, Mat Perino, Michael Sable

(Not pictured: Stephanie Brennan, Esther Hause, Steve Powell, Connie Vickers)

GERTRUDE BURNS ELEMENTARY SCHOOL
Newcastle, Weston County, Wyoming
(1960 – 1961)

Students: 1st Row: Barbara Honodel, April Manders, Betty Burr, Mary Jo Zanoni, Mary Ratigan, Aleta Martin, Kathy Wake, Joyce Beardsley, Cecilia Thomas, Nancy Franz

                      2nd Row: Dean Procunier, Eddie Humes, Steven Smith, Judy Hardy, Merille Miller, Ricky Naramore, Tony Skufca John Halsey

                      3rd Row: Casey Ward, Mike Patton, Hedley Carbis, Ronald Erdman, Benjamin Ayres

GERTRUDE BURNS ELEMENTARY SCHOOL
(1961 – 1962)

Gertrude Burns – 1961-62 – Heptner – Grade 2

Students: 1st Row: Dennis Williamson, Lynn Anderson, Bobby Miller, Johnnie Olds, Kenneth Jones, Jeanne Schultz, Mike Porter

            2nd Row: Debra Hecker, Gary Lamb, Sheila Loebs, Randy Kouf, Tia Welch, Donald Berdahl, Jackie Campbell**

            3rd Row: Ricky Farris, Lori Taylor, Chris Hansen, Debbie Case, Frank Henderson, Donna McDaniel, Kim Elliott

(Not pictured: Mike Kozisek, Donna Case)

(Student Teacher: Jean Smith)

**Jeanette taught Jackie, who was blind, how to read and write Braille and to type on the typewriter.

263

GERTRUDE BURNS ELEMENTARY SCHOOL
(1962 – 1963)

Students: 1st Row: Mike Holst, Kevin Bertagnolli, Becky Highland, Carol
                           Dilts, Pat Brennan, Bettie Henderson, Gerry Carr, Ray
                           Schmolt, Toby Rhoads, Dale Kauffman, Randy Farella,
                           Billie Ann Boulden
              2nd Row: Linda Naramore, Teena Cool, Stacy Thorpe, Gary Fall,
                           Pam Macy, LouAnn Erickson, Kathy Shook, Jalene King,
                           Bobby Nagle, Michele Smith, Dennis Ackley, Mike Scissons

(Student Teacher: Janet Lynn)

GERTRUDE BURNS ELEMENTARY SCHOOL
(1963 – 1964)

Students:

Stanley Butolph	Linda Howard	Rachelle Powell
Rebecca Clark	Steven Hull	Stephanie Reutner
James Cook	Debbie Kiesling	Bradley Self
Patricia Ebert	Sandra Mangus	Kevin Stepusin
Douglas Goodart	John Murphy	Sharon Stewart
Michael Henry	Steven Phillips	Carmel Tanner
Robert Hockett	Barry Phillips	Brian Weeg

(Student Teacher: Louise Trowe)

GERTRUDE BURNS ELEMENTARY SCHOOL
(1964 – 1965)

(Jeanette did not have a list of names for these students)

(Student Teacher: Marilyn Rahmig)

GERTRUDE BURNS ELEMENTARY SCHOOL
(1965 – 1966)

(Jeanette did not have a list of the names for these children)

(Student Teacher: Linda Porter)

GERTRUDE BURNS ELEMENTARY SCHOOL
(1966 – 1967)

Students:

Timothy Ayres	Connie Dunn	Jeffrey Lincoln
Eddie Billings	Tresa Gorsuch	Debora Marquiss
Joseph Cash	Steven Hitshew	Jodie McCoy
Stephen Colich	Russell Hockett	Brett Self
Jolene Coy	Deloris Howell	Judy Soenksen
Linda Cummings	Jamie Jones	Mark Winland
Stephen Curtis	Michael Larson	Marie Wrightson

(Student Teacher: Carol Cook)

GERTRUDE BURNS ELEMENTARY SCHOOL
(1967 – 1968)

(Jeanette did not have the names of these children)

(Student Teacher: Wanda Drake)

GERTRUDE BURNS ELEMENTARY SCHOOL

[Note from compiler: A list of the children or a class photograph was not found in Jeanette's photograph collection of classes for the following years:

(1968 – 1969)   Student Teacher: Jeanne Love
(1969 – 1970)   Student Teacher: Sue Riggs
(1970 – 1971)
(1971 – 1972)
(1972 – 1973)
(1973 – 1974)
(1974 – 1975)
(1975 – 1976)
(1976 – 1977)

Jeanette retired from teaching on June 29, 1977.

PART FOUR

THEIR RETIREMENT YEARS
(1977 - 2001)

Jeanette and Leona Heptner
(August 1984)
(Taken in Leona's garden at 412 Circle Drive, Gillette, Wyoming)

About six weeks before Jeanette's resignation on June 29, 1977, from teaching at the Gertrude Burns Elementary School in Newcastle, Wyoming, their brother, Oscar Herman Heptner, died. He passed away on May 5, 1977, in Newcastle, Wyoming, from cancer. Jeanette sold her house in Newcastle and moved back to Gillette to live with her sister Leona at 412 Circle Drive. Leona had retired from teaching in June 1975. There they began new lives without teaching. They shared their lives pursuing similar interests in their church, their lodge, sororities, and other clubs. Interspersed with these, they began traveling. They organized the Emergency Closet (TEC Shop) sponsored by the First Presbyterian Church. The Campbell County Council of Community Services recognized their work for the TEC Shop on October 20, 1981, for their outstanding and unselfish cooperation with the Council in helping provide for human needs in the community.

Jeanette joined the Stitch and Skillet Club at its Christmas party held at Irene Whisler's home in December 1977. Now all three sisters were members of the club sponsored by the Campbell County Extension Office. They participated in the County Fair with their handiwork, garden produce, canned and fresh vegetables, baked goods, etc. They, along with the other clubs, manned the exhibit booth during the County Fair each year.

On January 6, 1979, their remaining brother, Eugene John Heptner, died suddenly. He was spending the winter in town with Leona and Jeanette, and he passed away there at home with them. They felt a great emptiness with both brothers passing away so close together. Leona and Jeanette have special memories of their lives together, working, playing as youngsters, their camping and fishing excursions, and their many card games (especially Crazy Eights, Seven-Up, Canasta, and the never ending game of cribbage). Eugene and Oscar always had a game of cribbage going that never seemed to end. They always just picked it up where they stopped, leaving the cribbage board on the corner of the dining room table until the next time. Their oldest sister, Irene Lydia Heptner Whisler, passed away November 5, 1983, at the Pioneer Manor from complications of skin cancer. Slim Whisler, their brother-in-law, had passed away five months earlier on June 7, 1983, at Campbell County Memorial Hospital after a lengthy illness with heart disease. The loving care and attention Leona and Jeanette paid to their sister and brother-in-law gained them the eternal gratitude of their nieces Lorna and Olive Whisler. They, at that time, were living and working in the Washington, D. C., area and were unable to spend no more than two to three weeks in Gillette at any one time. With these losses, Leona and Jeanette carried on, along with Dorothy Whisler Heptner, as the Heptner family senior members. Leona and Jeanette unhesitantly acted as surrogate parents to their nieces and nephew as the years continued to spin by.

Leona and Jeanette did a lot of traveling, starting with their first trip to London, England, and Paris, France, in September 1977, with Carolyn Oedekovan and Nora Perkins. In March 1978, they took a bus tour of the southwest, which came to an end for Jeanette and Leona when Jeanette became ill and was hospitalized in El Paso, Texas. She spent eleven days at the El Paso Hospital before being transferred to the Weston County Memorial Hospital, Newcastle, Wyoming. However, she soon recovered, and they signed up for a Canada West Tour that began August 30, 1978. March 1979 found them again on the bus, this time their destination was Washington, D.C., and New York City.

August 1980 found them touring the southeast portion of the states. San Francisco, California, was their destination in the spring of 1981. That fall they toured the Great Lakes and northeastern fall colors. They took in the World's Fair in February 1982 and again that fall of September 1982 they were found heading for a tour of the Canadian Rockies. In April 1983, they were traveling through the southwest. That December they flew to Alexandria, Virginia, to spend Christmas with their nieces, Lorna and Olive Whisler. In 1984, they participated in several trips/tours with the Powder River Tour, such as: Winter Tour January 24-February 19; Mystery Tour August 30-September 2; Colorful Colorado Tour September 4-13th; and New England Tour September 25-October 16th.

In March 1985, they signed up for the Azalea Trip through the South, with stops in Disney World, Kennedy Space Center, and Nashville. One of their fellow travelers, H.M.C., wrote a poem about their trip.

REMEMBERING
(a poem written by a fellow traveler on their
March 1985 Spring Azalea Tour Down South.

Now what do we do when we retire?
Well, I'll tell you what we do.
We contact Annabell, Bonnie, and Don.
They plan a trip that tops them all.
We pay the price, and pack our bags.
We meet new friends and call them by name,
As if we'd known them years ago.

It's right side first and left side last—
Up one seat right and left side back.
It's candy time and juice break now.
Back on the bus and ready to go.
We'll stop at the Bluffs and be on our way,
To Minden, Nebraska and Abilene, Kansas,
With memories of *Ike* in War and Peace.
Then its Independence with Harry and Bess
And memories of a President tough and sincere.

Memphis next and Preseley's home,
Memories great to all.
To celebrate St. Patrick's Day
There were beautiful corsages from Betty and Don.
On to Vicksburg, a highlight event.
On we go—more sights to see.

Homes of the South in Antebellum Days—
Now that's a word we all must know.
"Before the Civil War"
They are unique, these homes of yore.
New Orleans, now who would forget
The tour of the city and paddlewheel ride,
Not even the rain could dampen these.
Bellingrath Gardens, Mobile's pride,
Would make Wyoming run and hide.
More celebrations, I should say.
Forty-five years of wedded bliss.
Newcomers have come to this.
Ocala, a dinner and a cake to cut.
Congratulations, Nellie and Ralph.
Causeways, horse farms, EPCOT, too.
(Experimental Prototype Community of Tomorrow)
Cyprus Gardens---beauty abounds.
Water show and tunnel cake—
Oh, my goodness! What a treat!

On to the Cape and Kennedy Center.
It was "Oh, my goodness"—"Oh, look there!"
"I can't believe it"—"Those rockets—how big!"
Here begins the History of Space.

St. Augustine----Oh so old!
The first in the old U. S.
The Fountain of Youth, we seemed to skip.
Thank you, Don, for a trip to the ocean

To find some shells and to wash our feet.
Andersonville, the Prison of Fate,
Civil War tortures all see med so great.
With Roosevelt memories imbedded in minds,
Made Warm Springs come alive,
And remind us of his greatness.

Atlanta next, with ahs and ohs.
Historical facts and modern growth,
Graces a city of beauty and charm.
Anxiety grew, as Nashville neared.
The Grand Ole Opry was near at hand,
Roy Acuff and Hank Snow, Box Car Willie and Jim Ed Brown.
All were there to please the crowd,
Who could care if the music was loud.

O, we weren't through by any means.
St. Louis and its Arch to see,
If those darn clouds would only clear.
But then instead, a whistle blew.
The Robert E. Lee put out its call,
On the Old Mississippi loud and clear,
"Come to our show and eat a bite—
we'll entertain you royally tonight."

Up and about---and yes, no rain.
To visit Becky, Tom, and Huck.
Their homes to see and caves to explore.
There were Mark Twain and Molly Brown
To help make up Hannibal Town.
Across the Missouri in rain and snow,
To reach Nebraska for a night's repose.
38 and snow on the ground,
A reminder of the Ole March Lion.
Little Duffer greeted us too.
Coffee tea, and breakfast for all.
"2 below" our Director said,
"Oh, Gee whiz---is it really?"
The rightful answer did come out.
"April Fool!" this Monday morning.
We reach the Bluffs, our last night out.
To bid adieu, to friends so true.

We thank you, Don. You are the best.
Mother Superior (Gee that's hard to rhyme)
So, Annabel, we thank you both.
Bonnie, all the plans you made,
We thank you very much.
Cecil, thanks for colds you helped
And the fallen ones we had.
Passing keys and candy canes,
And sharing stories and jokes,
We thank you, the folks who rode the bus.
It made our trip complete.
Thanks, *Betty Can*, co-pilot of our bus.
No, this really hasn't any rhyme,
But there's a reason, I admit.
I "writ" this Annabel,
For your scrap book memories,
And to record our Azalea Trip down South.

Upon their return, they prepared for a late May trip to Iowa to visit their cousins. Their niece, Lorna, flew to Rapid City, South Dakota, where they met her, and then she drove them to Iowa for a week's visit. On the return trip they went by way of Fort Laramie, Wyoming, as Lorna had never visited that Fort. They arrived at Lingle, Wyoming, on June 2, 1985, to attend the 50th wedding anniversary celebration of David and Marge Whisler. On June 13th, they went on another Powder River Mystery Tour weekend. August 9 – Sept 2nd they were traveling on the Glacier Park Tour. In February 1986 they flew to Alexandria, Virginia, to spend a few weeks helping Lorna celebrate her 50th birthday. While there they flew a commuter plane to New Jersey to visit with some long-time hunter friends. They had a most interesting detour flight on their way back to Virginia via Philadelphia, Pennsylvania!! From June 2-15th that same year they toured Alaska, Anchorage, Denali Park, Mt. McKinley, Fairbanks, Tok, Whitehorse, Skagway, and Ketchikan. They left Alaska on the ferryboat sailing along the glaciers on their way back to the states, stopping to visit Vancouver, British Columbia, Canada. While in Alaska, Leona won a ride on a sled pulled by dogs. Since this was summer in Alaska when there is no snow on the ground, the sled had tiny wheels so the dogs could pull it easily on the snowless ground. She enjoyed the ride immensely. They arrived back home with just enough time to wash clothes and repack for, first, a one-day Powder River Mystery Tour on July 15, 1985, and then in August they were off on the bus to meet a ferry at Portland, Maine, for a ferry crossing to Yarmouth, Nova Scotia. In 1987, they went on the Powder River Aspen Tour September 25-29, and then again beginning December 27th, they traveled to Pasadena, California, to attend the Rose Bowl Parade on New Year's Day 1988. They returned home on January 7, 1988. No tours in 1988 until the Continental Tours Haunted Halloween Tour, October 30-31st. In 1989, they signed up for the Continental Summer Suspense Tour, May 31, 1989; the Southern Circle Tour, October 28 to November 14, 1989; and the Christmas Festival Tour December 1-3, 1989.

During the summer of 1990, Lorna and Olive Whisler arrived in Gillette with their British friends, Jean and Erik Thacker, Margaret Griffith, and Debbie Thacker from Leeds, England. A nine-passenger van was rented and they all, including a bus driver and Leona and Jeanette, toured the Big Horn Mountains, Yellowstone National Park, Teton National Park, and the Black Hills, Mount Rushmore, and Devil's Tower. That year they also participated in the St. Patrick's Day Mystery Tour in March and the Christmas Festival Tour in December.

In March 1991, Leona and Jeanette moved once again into a house at 608 Ross Avenue. The house on Circle Drive had become a bit small for two retired school teachers and all their mementos from their individual teaching careers. The new home provided ample storage and room for them to separate; store, and display everything within easy reach for them. That November a Heptner mini-family reunion was held on Thanksgiving Day, November 28, 1991. Dorothy Heptner's 81st birthday was also celebrated that same day.

In 1992, they went on another three-day Mystery Tour April 30-May 2, to Ouray, Colorado, which as it turned out would be the last bus tour they would take.

Leona, with Jeanette and Eugene, continued to meet yearly with her *Round Robin* group. This group consisted of a few early rural northern Campbell County schoolteachers. The group began in 1942 when they started a *round robin* letter among themselves. They held their first get together in the summer of 1943. The letter exchange continued through the years. At a meeting in 1971, they added up the years of teaching experience which the group represented. More than 300 years of working with young people in class rooms were totaled. Another highlight that year was the appointment of Dr. Laurence Walker as head of the English Department at the University of Wyoming in Laramie. The group continued their yearly gatherings at someone's home each summer. Jeanette and Eugene also attended along with the spouses of the other members. The members include:

Mrs. Melissa Bing, of Gillette, Wyoming

Miss Leona Heptner, of Gillette, Wyoming

Mrs. Carolyn Oedekovan, of Gillette, Wyoming

Mrs. Beryl Smelser, of American Falls, Idaho

Mrs. Mary Anderson Stephens, of Battle Lake Minnesota

Mrs. Mary Street, of Gillette, Wyoming

Dr. Laurence Walker, of Laramie, Wyoming

Mrs. Dorothy Bailey Will, of Cheyenne, Wyoming

Mr. Oscar Will, of Cheyenne, Wyoming

These gatherings provided fellowship over shared food and drink, as they caught up on each family's news and shared their experiences in teaching in rural schools during the earlier days of Campbell County. It was easily the highlight event of each summer. As the years passed by, the group became smaller and smaller until they could no longer travel to meet due to age and illnesses.

With the opening of the new Campbell County Senior Citizen's Center on Stocktrail Avenue, Leona and Jeanette, in their spare time, took the opportunity to learn how to paint. They both took oil and pastel painting lessons provided at the Center. They soon became experienced enough to win ribbons at both the Campbell County Fair and the Wyoming State Fair. Jeanette also started pencil drawing and found she liked that about as well painting with oil.

Both Leona and Jeanette continued their work with the Rebekah Lodge. After moving back to Gillette, Jeanette transferred her membership from the Gateway Lodge in Newcastle to the Jewel Lodge No 28 in Gillette on December 21, 1978. Leona was installed as Noble Grand in 1976 and Jeanette in 1982. Leona was elected District Deputy President for two years. She was elected treasurer in 1980, a position she held until 2000. Leona also served as President of District Nine of which the Jewel Rebekah Lodge is a member from 1987 to 1989. Jeanette was also elected as District Deputy President in 1983. On November 13, 1988, the Jewel Rebekah Lodge No. 28 honored Leona and Jeanette with the Decoration of Chivalry, the highest honor given by this Lodge.

It was an evening enjoyed by the honorees and the members of their family who were invited as their honored guests. Darrell Heptner served as his Aunt Leona's escort, and Robert Prazma served as his Aunt Jeanette's escort. Dustin and Derek Cooper, Ashley and Allyson Sicks served as attendants. Their niece, Lorna Whisler, flew in from Alexandria, Virginia, to surprise them as they came in the door of the Rebekah Lodge.

The 1990s brought many happy events including several short bus tours, branding day at Darrell's, visits from nieces and nephews, etc. Health problems began to slow them down physically from Jeanette's heart surgery in February 1994 to Leona's leg/nerve problems in 1997. After spending some time in the Pioneer Manor, they were able to return to their home with in-home care services. Vera Hall, Carol Van-Rensellaer and Donna Geiser were hired to assist them during the day from 8:00 am until 6:00 pm. These ladies allowed Leona and Jeanette to continue pursuing their various lodge and sorority meetings, take day trips to Sheridan, the Devil's Tower, the Black Hills, and south to Fort Casper, or just to the parks around Gillette for a picnic lunch.

On March 1, 2000, Jeanette celebrated her 80th birthday, and on August 2, 2000, Leona celebrated her 88th birthday. Leona died on January 13, 2001; Jeanette on December 5, 2002. Both were buried at Pleasant Valley Cemetery, Rozet, Wyoming.

Jeanette and Leona Heptner about to board the Powder River bus to begin one of their many tours during the 1980s

Carolyn Oedekovan, Leona and Jeanette Heptner on board the M/S Scotia Prince which ferried them across to Portland, Maine, from Marmouth, Nova Scotia, 1985

TETON NATIONAL PARK
Summer 1990
Lorna Whisler, Jeanette and Leona Heptner, Debbie Thacker,
Olive Whisler, Jean Thacker, Eric Thacker, Margaret Griffith
The Thackers and Margaret Griffith were Lorna's friends from Leeds, England.
Jean and Lorna have been *pen pals* since 1953.

Leona and Jeanette Heptner
At Fort Fetterman's Gift Shop

1997
THE DECORATION OF CHIVALRY
PRESENTED TO LEONA AND JEANETTE
ON
NOVEMBER 13, 1988
By the Jewel Rebekah Lodge No. 28, Gillette, Wyoming

THE DECORATION OF CHIVALRY

It has a cross of ancient design—made of white
Enamel—white signifying JUST;

The cross is embedded in a frame of gold—
Gold signifying HONORABLE;

Mounted on the face of the cross—a heart of
Scarlet—scarlet signifying MERCIFUL;
And a crown signifying BRAVE.

On the back of the Jewel is the motto:
BE JUST; BE MERCIFUL, BE HONORABLE; BE BRAVE.

This jewel is suspended from a golden pin, in the center of which is a beautiful diamond symbolic of the light of the Brotherhood of Man, its rays shedding happiness over the entire World.

LEONA AND JEANETTE
WITH THEIR SPECIAL GUESTS
(November 13, 1988)

Don Cooper, Marleen Cooper, Audrey Heptner, Shirley Prazma,
Jeanette Heptner and Derek Cooper, Robert Prazma, Leona Heptner,
and Dustin Cooper, Corina Allen, Dorothy Heptner, Darrell Heptner, and Lorna Whisler

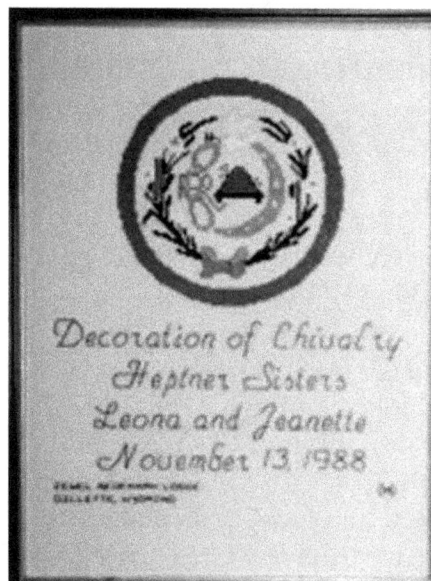

(Stitched by Lorna J. Whisler)

Leona Heptner and some of her paintings at the
Campbell County Senior Citizen's Center
(1980s)

Jeanette Heptner and some of her paintings at the
Campbell County Senior Citizen's Center
(1980s)

ROUND ROBINS GATHERING - August 1966

Back Row: Melissa Bing, Beryl Smelser, Carolyn Oedekovan, Leona Heptner
Mary Anderson Stephens, Laurence Walker, Mary Street

MEMBERS AND GUESTS

Back Row: Jeanette Heptner, Dorothy Will, George Oedekovan, _____ Street, Laurence Walker,
Oscar Will, Jim Bing, and Eugene Heptner
Front Row: Beryl Smelser, Melissa Bing, Mary Anderson Stephens, _____ Walker,
Mary Street, Carolyn Oedekovan, and Leona Heptner

ROUND ROBINS MEET 26TH TIME - 1969

A jolly group of former rural Campbell County teachers gathered Sunday for their 26th annual meeting at the home of Mr. and Mrs. George Oedekovan. The wives and husbands of the teachers also were present to enjoy the visiting and noon picnic lunch. This year the entire group was present. Seated are: Mrs. Mary Street of Gillette; Mrs. Mary Anderson Stephens of Battle Lake, Minnesota; Miss Leona Heptner and Mrs. Melissa Bing, both of Gillette; and Mrs. Dorothy Will of Cheyenne, Wyoming. Standing are: Dr. Laurence Walker of Laramie, Wyoming; Mrs. Carolyn Oedekovan of Gillette; Mrs. Beryl Smelser of American Falls, Idaho; and Oscar Will of Cheyenne, Wyoming. (*The News Record,* Gillette, WY, Thursday, August 7, 1969).

608 Ross Avenue, Gillette, Wyoming

THE HEPTNER FAMILY *SENIOR* MEMBERS
Thanksgiving Day, November 28, 1991

Standing: Olive Whisler, Lorna Whisler, Shirley (Heptner) Prazma,
Darrell Heptner and Darleen Heptner
Sitting: Dorothy (Whisler) Heptner, Jeanette Heptner, and Leona Heptner

Jeanette and Leona Heptner
(1997)

LONG TIME *SPECIAL* FRIENDS
Leona Heptner, age 82, and Carolyn Oedekovan, age 86.
(1998)

Wisdom for the Millennium

"Never give up. After each time that you get a setback, pick up and start again. There's always a better way."

Leona Heptner, 86
She moved to Gillette in 1914 with her family, who homesteaded nine miles north of Rozet. She taught at rural Campbell County schools and at Gillette schools for 44 years. She rode horseback each day from the homestead to her first teaching job at Cottonwood Creek School, which was north of the homestead about eight miles. "The ride was invigorating. I had to take care he didn't get loose from me at school because if he did, I wouldn't have a way to get home."

Serving you since 1971 into the Millennium.

CAMPCO FEDERAL CREDIT UNION
902 E. 3rd • Gillette, WY • 682-6105

From the *News-Record*, Gillette, Wyoming, April 18, 1999

Wisdom for the Millennium

"Don't give up. Keep working. Analyze your accomplishments. Pick out what's good and carry on."

Jeanette Heptner, 79
She was born at the family homestead north of Rozet and taught for more than 30 years after graduating from CCHS in 1939. Teaching seemed an appropriate career. "It was the only thing we could get into way back then," she said. But she also likes to learn, recently learning how to operate a computer and communicate via e-mail on the Internet.

Keeping you informed into the Millennium...

The News-Record
Serving Gillette since 1904

From the *News-Record*, Gillette, Wyoming, April 22, 1999

289

Leona Sophia Heptner
(1912 - 2001)

Jeanette Louise Heptner
(1920 - 2002)

As for man,
his days are as grass:
as a flower of the field,
so he flourisheth.
For the wind passeth over it,
and it is gone.
But the mercy of the Lord
is from everlasting
to everlasting.

Psalms 103

(Pictures copied from their Funeral Memorial brochures;
scripture copied from Jeanette Heptner's Memorial brochure)

Legacy of the Heptner Sisters

It has not been determined how many children Leona and Jeanette taught in those elementary school classes during their combined eighty years of teaching; mostly first and second grade classes. Both began their teaching years in small remote rural schools in Campbell and Crook counties and ended in larger more modern schools in the cities of Gillette and Newcastle, Wyoming. Their love of guiding young minds along their paths to adulthood carries on today. Because they considered themselves blessed with many opportunities they established the following:

Leona S. and Jeanette L. Heptner Scholarship Fund
University of Wyoming, Laramie, Wyoming

Established May 16, 1995, to make scholarship grants to students enrolled in the College of Education, University of Wyoming. To be eligible for this scholarship award, applicants must major in general elementary education and have successfully completed at least two years of undergraduate study or be a graduate or returning student. Financial need, as determined by the Office of Student Financial Aid, shall be a criterion. Having met these requirements, first preference shall be given to applicants who are residents of Campbell County, Wyoming; second preference to residents of Wyoming outside Campbell County; and third preference to out-of-state students.

Jeanette L. Heptner Scholarship
Northern Wyoming Community College Scholarship Fund
Sheridan, Wyoming

Jeanette L. Heptner Scholarship was established in 1996 to honor Jeanette's contributions to the college. She attended school in Campbell County. She was trained as a teacher at the University of Wyoming and other schools. Then she taught in rural or small city schools in Big Horn, Campbell, Crook, and Weston counties. This scholarship assists nursing and computer technology students at both Sheridan and Gillette Colleges.

Yellowstone Academy
Heptner Education Center
Yellowstone Boys and Girls Ranch
Billings, Montana

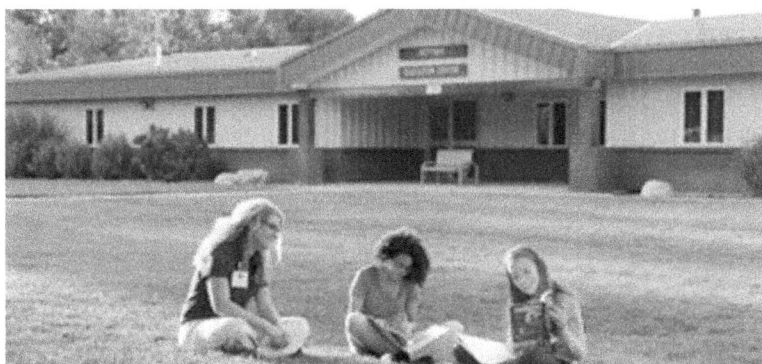

Heptner Educcation Center

Here at this academy, youth in residential care as well as students needing support from surrounding school districts receive educational programming through the Yellowstone Academy. The academy offers regular education, special education, vocational education, and other services. It operates year-round on a trimester academic calendar. Average age of students ranges from ten through whatever age they complete High School.

291

Heptner Cancer Center
Campbell County Memorial Hospital
Gillette, Wyoming

In memory of their brothers, Eugene and Oscar and their sister, Irene, they contributed monies toward the construction of an oncology center at the Campbell County Memorial Hospital. Construction began in June 2001, with Jeanette who with a frail set of hands helped to move the first scoops of dirt at its official ground-breaking ceremony. When it was opened on February 14, 2002, Leona and Jeanette were honored by the announcement of the center's name: Heptner Radiation Oncology Cancer Center. Today the name has been shortened to Heptner Cancer Center. The center provides advanced facilities and comprehensive cancer treatment as a branch of Campbell County Memorial Hospital, as well as programs including chemotherapy and radiation therapy for patients in Gillette and northeast Wyoming.

(The *News Record*, Gillette, Wyoming, Vol 97 No. 133 Thursday, June 7, 2001; The *News Record*, Gillette, Wyoming, Sunday February 24, 2002; Notes of Jeanette Heptner undated)

Appendix A

A Brief History of the

David Riley and Pearl Vida (Duvall) Whisler

Family

David Riley and Pearl Vida (Duvall) Whisler Family

May 1919, Mayberry, Pawnee County, Nebraska
Dorothy, Elmer, Riley, holding Leonard, David, Vida, Carroll *Slim*, Ashton *Ton*

David Riley *Riley* Whisler was born June 14, 1882, in Smartsville, Johnson County, Nebraska, to Henry and Adell (Crandall) Whisler. Pearl Vida was born October 7, 1887, in David City, Butler County, Nebraska, to Richard and Catherine (Slade) Duvall. Riley and Vida were married on October 4, 1904, in Tecumseh, Johnson County, Nebraska. Riley rented farms in Johnson and Pawnee counties until he moved his family to Wray, Yuma County, Colorado, in 1919.

Carroll *Slim*, holding Leonard, Dorothy, Vida, David, Ashton *Ton*,
and Elmer Wray, Yuma County, Colorado, summer 1920

Dry weather caused Riley, in 1922, to drive north in his Model T truck with his three older sons, Carroll, Elmer, and Ashton, to look for land to homestead. He obtained a quitclaim homestead from Raymond George located seven miles north of Rozet along the Adon Road and Cottonwood Creek. The homestead's location was Section 2, Township 50 North, Range 70 West, and Section 35, Township 51 North, Range 70 West.

Vida and the younger children moved from Wray, Colorado, to Rozet in 1923. Upon arrival the family first stayed with Vida's mother, Catherine (Slade) Duvall Clark, known throughout the Rozet community as *Grandma Clark*. Riley rented the Frank George place northeast of Rozet along the Well Creek Road now known as the South Heptner Road for his family to live in while he proved up on the homestead. The house was big enough to accommodate Riley and Vida's large family. Vida Whisler's brother, James Duvall, had already homesteaded about three miles southeast of Rozet a few years earlier. And James and Vida's mother, Catherine Slade Duvall Clark, and her third husband, Daniel William Clark, also lived nearby. In the fall of 1923 Slim, after a disagreement between himself and his father, left for Anselmo, Custer County, Nebraska, to work for the Robert Poor family shucking corn. Two children were born to Riley and Vida at Rozet, Wyoming.

The George Place - 1924

Whisler Homestead – about 1925

Vida & Riley at the George Place
1925

Riley and Vida were the parents of sixteen children, ten lived to adulthood

Carroll Duvall *Slim*	born October 2, 1905, Tecumseh, Johnson County, Nebraska, who married Irene Heptner;
Elmer Dewey	born August 5, 1907, in Tecumseh, Johnson County, Nebraska, married Ruth Belle Johnson;
Ashton Alfred *Ton*	born January 21, 1909, in Tecumseh, Johnson County, who married Mildred Maurine Day;
Dorothy Catherine	born November 28, 1910, in Tecumseh, Johnson County, Nebraska, married Oscar Herman Heptner;
Laura May	born September 26, 1912, in Mayberry, Pawnee County, Nebraska, died December 17, 1915, in Tecumseh, Johnson County, Nebraska;
David R.	born October 11, 1914,.in Mayberry, Pawnee County, Nebraska, who married Marjorie Adell *Marge* Mayden;
Ross Jennings	born May 17, 1916, in Mayberry, Pawnee County, Nebraska, died: December 24, 1916, in Mayberry, Pawnee County, Nebraska;
Jess Willard	born: November 25, 1917, in Mayberry, Pawnee County, Nebraska, died: November 26, 1917, in Mayberry, Pawnee County, Nebraska;
Leonard Pershing	born October 18, 1918, in Mayberry, Pawnee County, Nebraska, who married 1st, Catherine *Kitty* Wolff, 2nd, Louise Harvey, 3rd, Mary Jean (Woods) Brownlee;
Joseph Adrain	born: August 16, 1919, in Mayberry, Pawnee County, Nebraska, died: January 13, 1920, in Mayberry, Pawnee County, Nebraska;
Josephine Adell	born: August 16, 1919, in Mayberry, Pawnee County, Nebraska, died: 1920 in Wray, Yuma County, Colorado;
Ellen Joan	born March 14, 1921, in Wray, Yuma County, Colorado, who married Lee Cummings;
Pauline Louise	born October 29, 1922, in Eckley, Yuma County, Colorado, who married Ferris Edwin Cook;
Dean Robert	born April 11, 1924, in Rozet, Campbell County, Wyoming, who married Helen May Kottraba; and
Evelyn Lillie	born May 22, 1926, in Rozet, Campbell County, Wyoming, who married Melvin Harvey Donner.

Sadly, Riley's plan for providing for his family on his homestead ended suddenly with his death on November 15, 1926, at the age of 44 from a massive heart attack while visiting a neighbor. Slim returned home to Rozet from Nebraska to help his mother work the homestead. Tragedy struck the family again, when on June 8, 1928, Vida also passed away from what the family later believed was complications of tick fever. This left Slim as the head of the remaining Whisler family, his brothers Ashton, David, Leonard, and Dean, his sisters, Dorothy, Ellen, Pauline, and Evelyn. Their brother, Elmer Whisler, was by then married to Ruth Johnson, with two children. Soon, however, Grandma Catherine Clark took Dean and Evelyn to live with her. Ellen went to live with her Uncle Jim and Aunt Elsie Duvall for a brief period eventually going to live with her sister Dorothy and brother-in-law Oscar Heptner. By 1936 upon the death of Grandma Clark, Evelyn joined Ellen and Pauline in the home of her sister, Dorothy and Oscar Heptner. Slim married Irene Heptner on July 2, 1930, and Leonard and Dean went to live with them on the Riley Whisler homestead. They attended school at the Deer Creek School about one mile north of the homestead. Riley and Vida are buried in the Pleasant Valley Cemetery, along the Miller Creek Road, northeast of Rozet, Wyoming.

Whisler Homestead – 1935
Home of Slim and Irene (Heptner) Whisler

THE WHISLER BROTHERS AND SISTERS

1936
Taken at the George Place after the death of Catherine (Slade) Duvall Clark, their grandmother.
Back Row: Slim, Ton, Dorothy, Elmer
Front Row: Leonard, Ellen, Evelyn, Dean, Pauline
(David is missing in photo)

Summer 1944 when Dean Whisler was home on leave
Back Row: Slim, Elmer, Ton, David, Leonard, Dean
Front Row: Dorothy Heptner, Ellen Cummings, Pauline Cook, Evelyn Whisler

Taken day of Slim Whisler's funeral June 1983
David Whisler, Evelyn Donner, Dean Whisler, Ellen Cummings
Ton Whisler, Pauline Cook, Leonard Whisler, Dorothy Heptner

The Whisler Family Tree

Five Generations

John Whisler
Born: 07 Apr 1800, Rockbridge Co, VA
Died: 26 Apr 1873, Appanoose Co, IA

Anna (Spitler) Whisler
Born: 04 May 1795, Botetcourt Co, VA
Died: 07 Nov 1885, Appanoose Co, IA

Buried: Fairview Cemetery, Udell, Appanoose County, Iowa

David Whisler
Born: 11 Nov 1836, Wayne Co, IN
Died: 16 Mar 1904, Clark Co, WA

Elizabeth Ellen (Miller) Whisler
Born: 28 Nov 1841, Putnam Co, IN
Died: 01 Apr 1935, Clark Co, WA

Buried: City Cemetery, Vancouver, Clark County, Washington

Henry Louis Whisler
Born: 08 Dec 1859, Appanoose Co, IA
Died: 01 Sep 1930, Pawnee Co, NE

Elizabeth Adell *Della* (Crandall) Whisler
Born: 26 Nov 1859, Tecumseh, Nebraska Territory
Died: 21 Nov 1955, Tecumseh, Johnson Co, NE

Buried: Lewiston Cemetery, Pawnee County, Nebraska

David Riley Whisler
Born: 14 Jan 1883, Johnson Co, NE
Died: 15 Nov 1926, Cambell Co, WY

Pearl Vida (Duvall) Whisler
Born: 07 Oct 1887, Butler Co, NE
Died: 08 Jun 1928, Cambell Co, WY

Buried: Pleasant Valley Cemetery, Rozet, Campbell County, Wyoming

The Children of
David Riley and Pearl Vida (Duvall) Family

Carrol Duvall *Slim*
(1905 - 1983)

Elmer Dewey
(1907 - 1968)

Ashton Alfred *Ton*
(1909 - 1994)

Dorothy Catherine
(1910 - 2001)

Laura May
(1912 - 1915)

David R.
(1914 - 1992

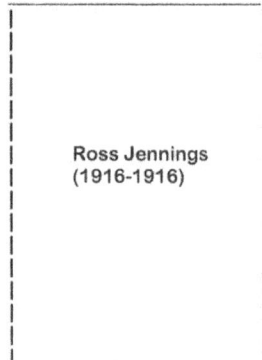

Ross Jennings
(1916-1916)

(Lived seven months)

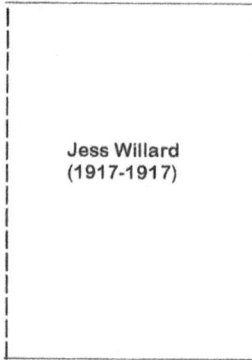

Jess Willard
(1917-1917)

(Lived one day)

Leonard Pershing
(1918 - 2003)

Joseph Adrian (1919-1920)
(Lived five months)
Josephine Adell (1919-1920)
(Lived about nine months)

Ellen Joan
(1921 - 2007

Helen Irene
(1922-1922)

(Died at birth)

Pauline Louise
(1922 - 1992

Dean Robert
(1924 - 2005)

Evelyn Lillie
(1926 - 2001)

Appendix B

Cottonwood Valley and Little Iowa Communities
Townships 50 and 51 North
Ranges 70 and 69 West
1928

RANGE 70 West	Range 69 West

Adon

Township 52 — Township 52

Speegle — Semlek

C. Donner — Harris-Simpson Livestock Company — Raudsep

D. O. Carsen White

Cottonwood Valley

R. Reed — Kuehne Brothers — *Little Iowa* — C. H. Simpson

Kuehne Brothers — J. Toro

Glover — **PV Cemetery**

F. Hamm — O. Woods — F. Thompson

McCurdy — Heptner C. Woods Ranney R. Woods G. Stull

Whisler — Shrand Weaver — M. Doane F. Jeffers

Township 51 — Woolsey Grunke **Township 51** Stewart

Hinds Fischer Doane — Shafer

Frank George — Stewart

Edith George — Kummerfeld

Johnson's

Jensen

O. Gray

Rozet

CB&Q — Shaughnessy 1903 — CB&Q

W === E

US 14-16 — School | Rozet — P.O. — US 14-16

Store

Rozet Cemetery

Township 50 — Township 50

Created by: Lorna J. Whisler, Aug 23, 2017
(Map is not to scale)
from Campbell County Assayer's Office 1928 Plat Maps

Acknowledgments

Photos of the Anton Heptner family were given to me by Leona Heptner shortly after I began researching the Heptner family in the late 1980s. The oldest pictures were taken in California, Moniteau County, Missouri, in the late 1890s. I think it is fair to assume they accompanied Frank to Iowa from Missouri and eventually in 1914 they were tucked along with various Young family photos safely in Grandma Heptner's trunk with other family mementos when she left Iowa on that emigrant train for Wyoming. Later occasional letters and pictures of Frank's brothers and sisters helped to put that family together. They all lived in and around Visalia, Tulare County, California. This tells us that Frank did communicate with them after he made the move to Wyoming, although he did not speak of them often with his children.

Most of the narrative for the Heptner family in this book came from Jeanette Heptner's chronological notes covering 1914-1998 and from the notebook SHE put together in the 1990s containing not only typed stories from when she was a girl but also from when she taught school, including pictures and lists of students for most of her classes. After she became ill and could no longer work on *her* story she gave it to me to finish. From this notebook came much of the minute details about the Heptner family's life during the first twenty years that I otherwise would not have known. Aunt Leona also had written a short biography and had saved photos and class rolls of most of her classes she taught.

Jeanette did not identify the names of the children in her second-grade classes that she taught at Cowley Elementary School, Cowley, Wyoming, 1951-1954. Wayne Holyoak, a student of hers in her 1952-1953 2rd grade class, with some help from former classmates, identified most of the children. Thank you, Wayne.

Other pictures of both Leona and Jeanette's classes did not have years indicated. Hopefully I have matched the pictures and children with the correct years, based on enrollment lists. But I may have recorded some in the wrong years. For that I can only humbly apologize.

Other family pictures chosen for this book came from a portion of the Leona and Jeanette Heptner collection that I inherited from Aunt Jeanette after she passed away and from my father, Slim Whisler, who was given a black box Kodak camera when he was about 12 years old. Without them this book would not reflect their histories correctly.

The brief history on the Whisler family was compiled from a book I put together for our first Whisler Family Reunion in 1993, held at the Dalby Fishing Park, Gillette, Wyoming. Photos for early ancestors were found on the Internet.

The farm record journals and 5-year diaries in various formats that my father, Slim Whisler, kept from 1926 through 1998, provided verification of certain events and conditions.

Without the guidance and editing by my good friend, Theresa Flaherty, this book would not be complete. Her patience with me, a grammar school failure, is appreciated beyond words.

Lorna J. Whisler
Natural Bridge, Virginia

NAME INDEX

A

Ackley, Dennis, 264
Ackley, Loren, 258
Acton, Bob, 248
Acton, Jim, 249,252
Addision, Russell, 209
Addison, Donna Renee, 211
Addison, Linnie Vondean, 209
Addison, Russell, 204
Addison, Sherryl Louise, 212
Addison, Vivian Ann, 204,209
Adon, Wyoming, 303
Adsit, Travis Lee, 219
Albers, Traci, 230
Albertson, Robert Dean, 207-208
Allen, Connie, 202,204
Allen, Corina Sue (Heptner), 132, 282
Allen, Danny, 258
Allen, Diana Gail, 212
Allen, Donald Edward, 202
Allen, Kathleen Ann Kathy, 257
Allen, Nancy Lee, 204
Allen, Neil Henry, 132
Allen, Norma Irene, 160
Allen, Pat, 260
Anderson, Betty Lou, 209,214
Anderson, Dawne Ree, 214
Anderson, John, 209, 214
Anderson, Louis, 257
Anderson, Lynn, 263
Anderson, Mary. *See* Stevens, Mary (Anderson)
Anderson, Miss Bertha Jane, 153
Anderson, Nicky Lynn, 209
Anderson, Robin Lee, 212
Anderson, Willis, 259
Appley, Judson, 202
Appley, Linda Laree, 202
Archer, Larry, 258
Archer, Wilhelmina *Minnie* (Heptner), 10, 12
Archer, Samuel Eugene, 10
Archer, Stephen, 260
Archibald, Betty, 157-158
Archibald, Elizabeth, 160
Archuleta, Anita, 208
Archuleta, Joe, 208
Archuleta, Max, 208
Archuleta, Orlando, 208
Arton, Roseann, 248
Asay, Leslie, 249
Asay, Linda, 251
Atkinson, Albert, 240
Atkinson, Anna, 240
Atkinson, Lionel, 240

Aulman, Harry E., 10
Ayres, Benjamin, 262
Ayres, Timothy, 268

B

Bailey, Frank, 209
Bailey, Robert Frank, 209
Bailey, Sybil, 209
Baird, Don, 248
Baird, Jane, 150
Baird, Jean, 150
Baird, Mrs., 43,150
Baird, Nancy, 150
Baity, Barbara, 216
Baity, Robert, 216
Baity, Jr., Robert Earl, 216
Baker, Hugh, 245
Baker, Jessie, 147
Baker, John, 245
Baker, Lawrence, 222
Baker, Ricky Dee, 222
Baker, Sherry, 222
Baker, Virginia, 157,160
Baley, Bertha, 222
Baley, John Eugene, 222
Baley, Ralph, 222
Ballard, Joseph Anthony, 213
Ballard, Peggy Sue, 219
Banks, Darlene, 252
Banks, Jack Howard, 216
Banks, James (?), 216
Banks, Joyce, 216
Barber, Scott, 227
Barlow, Janice Elaine, 212
Barnes, Elsie, 104
Bartsch, Mike, 260
Basch, Anna Elizabeth, 21, 25
Basch, Aunt Lydia (Young), 24-26, 58
Basch, Grace, 58
Basch, Herman, 21, 58
Basch, Johann, 25
Bates, Cynthia Anne, 209
Bates, Gertrude, 209
Bates, Karen Kay, 212
Bates, Richard, 209
Baughman, Allan Ray, 208
Baughman, Mable, 208
Baughman, Richard C., 204, 208
Bauman, Family, 101
Baumfalk, Danny, 199
Bay, Lilith, 157-158
Beaman, Dorothy Juanita, 158, 160
Beardsley, Joyce, 262
Beck, Bill, 101

Beck, Blanche, 101
Beck, Christian Henry, 15
Beck, Danny, 184
Beck, Iva Kay, 216, 218
Beck, Jerry, 216, 218
Beck, Larry, 184
Beck, Linda Lee, 213
Beck, Michael Francis, 216
Beck, Steven John, 218
Beckley, Arvella, 222
Beckley, Paul Wayne, 222
Begley, Maryetta, 256
Belamy, Gloria, 222
Belamy, Kurt, 222
Belferstone, Melvin, 214
Bell, Barbara, 209
Bell, John, 209
Bell, Nancy Lee, 209
Bellamy, Amber Gay, 222
Bengston, Esther, 216
Bengston, Richard Allen, 216
Bengston, Walter, 216
Bennett, Beverly Jean, 195
Bennick, Gay Diane, 202
Bennick, J. L. , 202, 214
Bennick, Jack, 204
Bennick, Junior, 157-158
Bennick, Junior L., 160
Bennick, Margo Ann, 204
Bennick, Ruth, 214
Bennick, Toby Lynn, 214
Berdahl, Donald, 263
Berdahl, Mark, 260
Berg, Kathleen Marie, 207
Bertagnolli, Kevin, 264
Bertoncely, Nancy Jean, 204
Bertoncely, Jr., Peter, 204
Betts, Condida, 228
Betts, Sharon, 228
Billings, Eddie, 268
Bills, Charlotte Roseanne, 209
Bills, Herbert, 209
Bills, Rosemarie, 209
Bing, James Allen, 219
Bing, Jim, 284
Bing, Melissa, 278, 284-285
Bingham, Peggy Sue, 218
Birdsall, Betty, 160
Blackley, J. C., 214
Blackley, Mike Carry, 214
Blackley, Ruth, 214
Blakely, Dean, 248
Blakely, Delia, 249, 251
Blank, Linda Lou, 252
Boehm, Aunt Emma (Young), 24, 26, 58
Boehm, Herman W., 21
Boehm, Martha, 21

Bolland, Don, 131
Bolsinger, Elmer, 159
Bond, Judy, 256
Bonne, Willie, 24
Booth, Shirley Didona. *See* McGraw, Shirley Didona (Booth)
Borne, Frederick Lee, 219
Boulden, Billie Ann, 264
Bradford, Clara, 218
Bradford, Johnny, 218
Bradford, Martha Jane, 218
Bradford, Rayburn, 218
Brandner, Betty L., 160
Brannan, Betty Lou, 214
Brannan, Rhonda, 214
Brannan, Richard Ernest, 213
Brannan, Wayne, 214
Bray, Larry Wayne, 195
Brennan, Nadine, 188
Brennan, Dick. *See* Brennan, Richard
Brennan, Dan, 99, 103
Brennan, Eileen, 71, 143-146
Brennan, Jerry, 191
Brennan, Jimmy, 191
Brennan, Mary, 70
Brennan, Nadine, 189
Brennan, Pat, 264
Brennan, Richard, 71, 144-145
Brennan, Stephanie, 261
Brewer, James, 195
Brewer, Jance Lea, 202
Brewer, L. O., 202
Bricker, Edna, 160
Bricker, Harold E., 145-146
Bricker, Louise, 147
Bridwell, Charlotte, 216
Bridwell, Debora Jean, 216
Bridwell, Robert, 193, 216
Briggs, Douglas Earl, 218
Brightly, Tookie, *See* Shidley, Tookie Brightly
Bringham, Homer, 218
Brower, Judy, 199
Brown, Louis, 259
Brown, Macil, 104
Brown, Robert Ervin, 207
Brown, Roger Kelly, 211
Brownlee, Mary Jean (Woods), 297
Brunson, Christina, 218
Brunson, David, 218
Brunson, Emma, 187-188, 245
Brunson, Winfred, 191
Bryant, Arlene, 245
Burdick, Floyd, 258
Burney, Denise Marie, 208
Burney, Hazel, 208
Burney, Ollie, 208
Burns, Ann Laura, 195
Burr, Betty, 262

Divis, Debbie Lynn. *See* McGraw, Debbie Lynn (Divis)
Doane, May, 303
Dolcater, Betty, 230
Dolcater, Robert, 230
Dolerena, Bessie, 158
Donner, Charlie, 117, 303
Donner, Dora, 117
Donner, Evelyn, 299
Donner, June, 176-177
Donner, Leone, 175-177
Donner, Melvin, 90
Donner, Melvin Harvey, 117, 297
Dorrington, George, 202
Dorrington, Steven George, 202
Doud, Deborah Kay, 212
Douglas, Robert, 218
Douglas, Sandra, 218
Downes, Alice, 209
Downes, Robert, 209
Downes, Robert Dorsey, 209
Doyle, Jack, 214
Doyle, Robert Phillip, 214
Doyle, Virginia, 214
Dozier, Jerry, 211
Drake, Judy, 198
Drake, Wanda, 236, 269
Drovdal, Douglas Arden, 209
Drovdal, Linda Jeanne, 214
Drovdal, Margaret Irene, 218
Drovdal, Norma, 214, 218
Drovdal, Norris, 209, 214, 218
Drovdal, Paul Andrew, 211
Duclo, Peggy, 260
Dunbar, James Martin, 222
Dunbar, Janice, 222
Dunbar, Joseph, 222
Duncan, Donald, 216
Dunn, Connie, 268
Duvall, Catherine (Slade). *See* Clark, Catherine (Slade) Duvall
Duvall, Elsie, 298
Duvall, Fred, 156
Duvall, Helen, 179
Duvall, James, 72, 116, 156, 296
Duvall, Jim, 116, 298
Duvall, Johnny, 188-189
Duvall, Miss Helen, 156
Duvall, Nadine, 184-186
Duvall, Pearl Vida. *See* Whisler, Pearl Vida (Duvall)
Duvall, Richard, 295
Duvall, Verlin, 184-185
Dybwad, David, 259
Dyer, Shirley Ann, 207

E

Early, Mary Ann, 13
East, Romona, 260
East, Sandra, 258

Eberhardt, Anna, 13
Eberhardt, Benedict, 13
Eberhardt, Daniel, 13
Eberhardt, Eddie, 10
Eberhardt, Elizabeth (Hagi), 10, 13-14
Eberhardt, Frank E., 13
Eberhardt, Frederick, 13
Eberhardt, Jacob, 13
Eberhardt, Johannes, 13
Eberhardt, John, 13
Eberhardt, John Henry, 13
Eberhardt, Lena. *See* Isenhart, Lena (Eberhardt)
Eberhardt, Mary, 9-10, 12
Eberhardt, Nicholas, 9-10, 13-14
Eberhardt, William, 13
Ebert, Patricia, 265
Eddy, Betty, 209
Eddy, Carol Dee, 209
Eddy, Lonnie, 209
Edelman, Mary, 227
Edleman, Anthony, 230
Edleman, Catherine, 230
Edleman, Patricia, 230
Edmison, Barbara Joy. *See* Heptner, Barbara Joy (Edmison)
Edmondson, Carol, 198
Edmunds, Alfred, 209
Edmunds, Ruth Mae, 209
Edmunds, Thomas Allen, 209
Edwards, Daphne, 39, 112
Edwards, Harold, 193
Edwards, Henry *Deafie*, 39
Eisenbarth, Connie, 260
Ekis, Gary Lee, 207
Eldridge, Edward Wayne, 204
Eldridge, Jimmy, 193
Eldridge, Wayne, 204
Elliott, Judy, 259
Elliott, Kim, 263
Engler, Michael, 233
Engstrom, Opal, 157
Erdman, Ronald, 262
Erickson, Larry, 259
Erickson, LouAnn, 264
Ernst, Blanche, 39, 54, 59
Ernst, David, 39, 54
Ernst, Genevieve, 39, 54
Ernst, C. R., 202
Ernst, Lois, 54
Ernst, Robert Harold, 202
Ettle, Beverly, 216
Ettle, Dale, 216
Ettle, Junetta Ruth, 216
Ewing, Virl, 193
Eyre, Don, 249, 252
Eyre, James, 207
Eyre, Rhonda, 213

F

Faas, Eugene, 193
Fahler, Lillian, 104
Fair, Florence, 141
Fall, Gary, 264
Fall, Jimmy, 258
Farella, Randy, 264
Farnsworth, Patty, 260
Farris, Ricky, 263
Ferguson, Daneen Joy, 213
Ferguson, Klara Rose L., 160
Field, Thomas Bradford, 213
Fischer, place, 41, 56-57, 70, 99, 138, 150
Fischer, Anita Lynn, 209
Fischer, Chuck, 208
Fischer, Dalene Marie, 208
Fischer, Diane. *See* McGraw, Diane (Fischer)
Fischer, Evelyn, 209
Fischer, Gayl D'Ann, 207
Fischer, Henry, 209
Fischer, Jesse, 303
Fischer, Judy Elaine, 207
Fischer place, 41, 56-57
Fish, Anthony, 230
Fish, Janice, 230
Fish, M. Lee, 230
Fisher, Mary, 208
Fisher, Melba, 157-158
Fitch, Douglas, 213
Fitch, Norma, 147
Fittrol, Jackie, 189, 191
Fittrol, Teddy, 191
Fitzpatrict, Cindy, 260
Flack, Martin, 210
Flack, Paulette, 210
Flamm, Donald, 216
Flamm, Meda, 216
Flamm, Rita Jean, 216
Fleck, Curtis Lee, 211
Fleck, Donad Raymond, 210
Fleck, Timothy Francis, 207
Foley, Eileen, 147
Force, James, 158-159
Force, James G., 160
Ford, Billy. *See* Ford, William Warren
Ford, Charlotte Darlene. *See* Heptner, Charlotte Darlene (Ford)
Ford, Terry, 199
Ford, William Warren, 257
Forrest, Bob, 214
Forrest, Lois, 214
Forrest, Loralei, 214
Forsha, Jeri Ann, 210
Forsha, Bill, 204, 210
Forsha, Jane, 158
Forsha, John Alan, 204
Forsha, June, 157, 160

Forsha, Marie, 210
Foster, Agnes Elizabeth. *See* McGraw, Agnes Elizabeth (Foster)
Foster, Arthur, 259
Fowler, Charles, 256
Fox, Zana Kay, 207
Franklin, Marvin Ennis, 219
Franz, Nancy, 262
Franzen, Becky, 227
Franzen, Wayne, 227
Frasier, Lucille, 214
Frasier, Melvin, 214
Frasier, Melvin Lee, 214
Frederick, Mildred Jule, 195
Freer, Donnie, 193
Freer, Fern, 157-158
Freer, Fernade M., 160
Freese, Barbara Jean, 213
Frick, Dorothy, 216, 218
Frick, Gerald Dwaine, 218
Frick, James, 216, 218
Frick, James Herman, 216
Frisbee, Bonnie Ray, 202
Fritz, John, 19
Frost, David, 248
Fulton, Phyllis, 179
Fulton, Tommy, 259

G

Gaddis, Deanna, 193
Gallbreathe, Loraine, 160
Galloway, Donald Lee, 257
Gardner, Donnie Ray, 219
Gardner, Laine, 71, 103, 143-146
Gardner, Mary, 70
Garman, Ronnie, 212
Garrett, Rocine, 147
Garrett, Tom, 99
Garvey, Jr., James Russell, 211
Gates, Cecelia, 222, 228
Gates, George, 222, 228
Gates, Paul Edward, 222
Gates, Tarla, 228
Gates, Thomas Jefferson, 216
Geer, Harl G., 157-158, 160
Geise, Adolph, 15
Geiser, Donna, 278
Gelock, Bob, 249
George, place, 116-117, 296
George, Edith, 137, 139, 303
George, Edwin, 147
George, Frank, 117, 303
George, Jack, 208
George, Jean, 208
George, Richard Marion, 208
George, Sally, 249
Gerlach, Lolynn, 213

Gifford, Clara, 249
Gilbace, Mary Gayl, 160
Glabaugh, Grace Carol, 160
Glearey, Cora, 160
Gleason, Gary Gene, 211
Glenney, Cora, 157-158
Glover, Bill, 240
Glover, George, 303
Glover, Jill, 227
Glover, Joyce, 240
Glover, Mrs., 240
Goodart, Douglas, 265
Gore, Emily, 256
Gorsuch, Tresa, 268
Gossett, Carl, 230
Gossett, Emma Lou, 230
Gossett, Frances, 230
Graham, Barbara Jo, 213
Graham, Brett, 227
Gray, Betty, 188
Gray, Cynthia, 212
Gray, O'Neal, 303
Gray, Russell, 240
Green, Christopher, 21
Green, Harl, 159
Green, Jeanette, 230
Green, M. L., 230
Green, Mark, 230
Green, Renee Janice, 213
Greer, James, 157
Greer, Jr., Charles, 160
Gregersen, Oluf, 104
Gregg, Robert, 199
Grey, Dorothy, 187-188
Griffith, Margaret, 277, 280
Griffith, Ronnie, 233
Grunke, Paul, 42, 303
Gulley, Cecilia, 259
Gulley, Donald, 214, 218
Gulley, Dorothy, 214, 218
Gulley, Gary, 260
Gulley, Kay Lorene, 219
Gulley, Rebecca Anne, 218
Gulley, Sue Ellen, 214
Gunter, Carol, 213
Gupton, Mary, 147

H

Hackett, Avis, 104
Haden, Kenneth E., 160
Hades, Kenneth, 158
Hagi, Benedick, 13, 14
Hagi, Elizabeth. *See* Eberhardt, Elizabeth (Hagi)
Haley, Robert, 193
Hall, Corder, 204
Hall, Dennis Tyler, 204
Hall, Vera, 278

Haller, Irene, 222
Haller, James, 222
Haller, Thomas Acquinas, 222
Halsey, John, 262
Hamilton, Vivian, 147
Hamm, Adolph, 39
Hamm, Alfred, 39, 139-142
Hamm, Bessie, 39, 139-142
Hamm, Beulah, 152
Hamm, Bob, 107
Hamm, Dorothy, 39, 139-142
Hamm, Evelyn, 112
Hamm, Fred L., 39, 303
Hamm, Gladys, 39, 139-142
Hamm, Mathilda Jane, 39
Hamm, Mildred, 39, 139-142
Hamm, Winifred, 39, 139-142
Hansen, Chris, 263
Hanslip, Mary, 177-178
Hanson, Gene Lyle, 212
Hanson, Michael Howard, 204
Hanson, Milford, 204
Hardin, William, 104
Hardy, Donna Rade, 208
Hardy, Howard, 208
Hardy, Judy, 262
Hardy, Kathleen, 208
Hardy, Kathleen Marie, 207
Haringer, Jackie, 259
Harlow, Bonnie Ruth, 195
Harlow, Kenneth, 199, 204
Harlow, Susan Myrtle, 204
Harmon, Bill, 216
Harmon, Don, 216
Harmon, Kyung, 216
Harmon, Lloyd, 214
Harmon, Vicki Louise, 214
Harms, Katherine, 15
Harned, Debra, 213
Harnett, Kevin, 228
Harnett, Lawrence, 228
Harnett, Sharon, 228
Harper, Gary Lee, 216
Harper, Maxine, 216
Harper, Wanda, 193
Harper, William J., 216
Harris, Hazel, 158, 159
Harris Simpson Livestock Company, 303
Harrod, David Bruce, 214
Harrod, Edwin, 199
Harrod, Jean, 222
Harrod, Jerry, 187
Harrod, LaVern T., 150, 157, 160, 218
Harrod, Lee, 195
Harrod, Lillian, 218
Harrod, Linda Anne, 218
Harrod, Loa Jean, 214

Kintz, Jim, 244
Kintz, Merna Jo, 244
Kinzer, Darlene, 217-218
Kinzer, Dick, 217
Kinzer, Lorie Lynn, 218
Kinzer, Mark Evan, 217
Kinzer, Richard, 218
Klug, Anna Marie, 204
Klug, Mark, 204
Knapp, Albert, 104
Knapp, Chris, 233
Knapp, Leslie Ray, 202
Knapp, Peggy Jo, 202
Knapp, Raymond, 199
Knigge, Gary, 230
Knigge, Gordon, 230
Knigge, Mary, 230
Knotts, Gary, 230
Knotts, Marshall, 230
Knotts, Patty, 230
Kock, Marilyn, 258
Koenig, David, 218
Koenig, Katherine, 218
Konig, Jacob Christian, 218
Kosderka, Alberta, 257
Kottraba, Edith, 222
Kottraba, Helen May, 117, 297
Kottraba, James, 222
Kottraba, Kathryn, 117
Kottraba, Ray, 117
Kottraba, Tammy Joan, 222
Kouf, Randy, 263
Kozisek, Mike, 263
Kreft, Ernest, 19
Kremers, Ed, 228
Kremers, Stephan, 228
Kremers, Theresa, 228
Kron, Robert Wayne, 219
Kuehne Brothers, 303
Kuehne, Carl, 39,54
Kuehne, Esther, 39
Kuehne, Esther Spencer, 54
Kuehne, Frank, 39, 54, 150
Kuehne, Marna, 39, 54, 150
Kummerfeld, Hans, 303
Kuntz, Lawrence, 228
Kuntz, Mark, 227
Kuntz, Pat, 228
Kuntz, Robin, 228
Kurht, Albert, 218
Kurht, Beverly, 218
Kurht, William Robert, 218
Kyte, Thomas, 207

L

LaCrosse, Ella Gertrude (Heptner), 10-12
LaCrosse, Harry, 10

Lajeunesse, Betty, 230
Lajeunesse, George, 230
Lajeunesse, Troy, 230
Lamb, Gary, 263
Lamb, Larry Allen, 257
Lamb, Virginia, 157-158
Landers, Lloyd, 158, 160
Lane, Kenneth, 213, 215
Lane, Raymond, 193
Lantham, Jimmy, 154
LaOrange, George, 218
LaOrange, Kathryn, 218
LaOrange, Thomas Jay, 218
Lara, Ben, 204, 208
Lara, Benerito, 202
Lara, Benny Wayne, 202
Lara, Donnie Ray, 204
Lara, Gloria Marie, 211
Lara, Rosa, 208
Lara, Rose, 204
Lara, William Kenneth, 208
Larsen, Chris, 101
Larsen, Hertha (Semlek), 170
Larsen, Marie, 101
Larson, Michael, 268
Latham, Mrs. Harold, 154
Latham, Richard, 258
Lawson, Gene, 256
Lawson, Jane, 158
Lee, Lonny Dee, 212
Leftus, Bob, 202
Leiker, Sheri, 233
Lelan, Darrell, 116
Lemons, Rosalie, 159
Lest, Luena, 224
Levison, Ella Mae, 204
Levison, Howard E., 204
Lewis, Betty, 157-158, 160
Lewis, Carolyn, 249
Lewis, John, 248
Lewis, Lorraine, 250252
Lewis, Reverend V. G., 160
Light, Charles Allen, 212
Lightman, Jerry, 258
Lillridge, Juanetta, 198
Lincoln, Jeffrey, 268
Linneman, Henry F., 204
Linneman, Larry Francis, 204
Litherland, Scherry, 261
Little Iowa, 303
Little, Mike, 249
Littleton, Ellenrose, 157-158
Loebs, Jack, 260
Loebs, Sheila, 263
Longtin, Joseph Duane, 130
Longtin, Kim (McGraw), 46, 130
Looby, Michael Thomas, 207

McGee, Tom, 157
McGee, Tom W., 160
McGee, Wilma, 179
McGraw, Sarah Beth, 130
McGraw, *Bunny. See* McGraw, Carlotta (Pisciotti)
McGraw, *Jerry. See* McGraw, Gerald Marvin
McGraw, *Nick. See* McGraw, Nicholas Shawn
McGraw, Agnes Elizabeth (Foster), 130
McGraw, Ashley Lynne, 130
McGraw, Bruce, 46, 161
McGraw, Bruce Lelan, 130
McGraw, Carlotta (Pisciotti), 130
McGraw, Darleen (Heptner). *See* Heptner, Darleen LaVonne (Heptner)
McGraw, David Jon, 130
McGraw, Debbie Lynn (Divis), 130
McGraw, Diane (Fischer), 130
McGraw, Dixie Jo, 130
McGraw, Eric Dean, 130
McGraw, Gerald, 131
McGraw Jr., Gerald Marvin *Jerry*, 46, 131
McGraw Sr., Gerald Marvin, 130
McGraw, Jan, 131
McGraw, Janet Marie (Rowley), 130
McGraw, Jennifer Joyce, 130
McGraw, Jeremy Thomas, 130
McGraw, Jerry. *See* McGraw Jr., Gerald Marvin
McGraw, Jordynn Arianna, 130
McGraw, Julia Ann (Jahnke), 130
McGraw, Jushua Michael, 130
McGraw, Kimmberlee Catherine *Kim. See* Longtin, Kim (McGraw)
McGraw, Merlyn, 46, 131
McGraw, Merlyn Keith, 130
McGraw, Michelle Lynn, 130
McGraw, Nicholas Shawn, 130
McGraw, Shirley Didona (Booth), 130
McGraw, Tabatha Dawn Marie, 130
McGraw, Jr., Gerald Marvin, 130
McGraw, Jr., Kyle Aaron, 130
McIntosh, Julie Claire, 219
McIntyre, Kenneth, 157
McKay, Paul, 259
McKenzie, Jean, 158, 160
McLaughlin, Alva George, 203
McLaughlin, Jesse Hugh, 211
McLaughlin, Katherine, 203
McLaughlin, Kathleen Elaine, 203
Mclelland, Janet Le, 218
McLeod, John, 130
McMahand, Donald Ray, 195
McMahand, Ronald Jay, 195
McMahon, Donna Lucille, 212
McMahon, Kathleen Theresa, 207
McMahon, Marie Louise, 204
McMahon, Tom, 204
McManamen, Jerry, 193

McMillan, Patricia Jane, 212
McVay, Jimmy, 258
Medlock, Suzy, 233
Meier, Herman, 25
Meppin, Bill, 116
Meppin, Lou (Young), 116
Meppin, William, 21
Meserve, Linda Ruth, 219
Messerly, Frederick, 13
Messerly, Rosanna, 13
Metzler, Ivan *Butch*, 257
Meyer, Deanne, 230
Meyer, Emma Sophia, 19
Meyer, Harlan, 230
Meyer, Lily, 230
Middagh, Larry Eugene, 257
Miller, place, 43
Miller, Bobby, 263
Miller, Carla Joan, 215
Miller, Clifford, 215
Miller, Conne Sue, 218
Miller, Craig, 224
Miller, Darlene, 215
Miller, Deborah Sue, 211
Miller, Dorse, 218
Miller, Elizabeth Ellen. *See* Whisler, Elizabeth Ellen (Miller)
Miller, Jeanie Raye, 203
Miller, Karen Ann, 219
Miller, Merille, 262
Miller, Rose, 218
Miller, Willard Eugene, 203
Mills, Cathy, 258
Mills, Clarabell, 244
Mills, Reynard, 244
Mindschenk, Janis, 259
Minser, John G., 204
Minser, Johnetta Lou, 204
Misch, Jimmy, 185
Mkenzie, Marian, 157
Momders, Robert, 224
Mondle, David Allen, 219
Monk, Barbara, 250
Monk, Nick, 249
Monk, Ronnie, 252
Montoya, Danny, 256
Moon, George, 70, 99
Moon, Russ, 70, 103
Moon, Russell, 99
Mooney, Allen, 199
Mooney, Dixie, 199
Mooney, Johnny, 195
Moore, Richard Derek, 210
Moran, Gilbert, 70, 99, 103
Moran, Neta, 148
Morgan, Barbara Jane, 211
Morgan, James, 157-158, 215
Morgan, Jean, 215

S

Thompson, Toby, 199
Thompson, Tommy Curtis, 215
Thompson, Wilbur *Bill*, 39
Thomson, Susan Lynn, 213
Thornton, Linda Lee, 211
Thorp, Lena, 179
Thorpe, Stacy, 264
Throne, Earl, 210
Throne, Ethel, 210
Throne, Stephen Thomas, 210
Tilson, Tommy, 193
Todd, Rae Ann, 211
Toland, John, 40
Toland, Ona, 40
Toland, Revend H. A., 39, 40
Toll, Myra Junann, 213
Tomingas, Arnold, 160
Tomingas, Henry R., 160
Toro, Elma, 155
Toro, John, 155, 303
Trowe, Louise, 236, 265
Tyrrell, Audrey, 210
Tyrrell, Charles Arlan, 207
Tyrrell, Janie Rae, 210
Tyrrell, Leo O., 204
Tyrrell, Roberta Dalene, 204
Tyrrell, Jr., Lee, 210

U

Uhl, Joann, 191
Underhill, Dale, 259
Underwood, Donna, 230
Underwood, Octa, 157-158, 160
Underwood, Russel, 230
Underwood, Sheila, 230
Unruh, Ercell, 215
Unruh, Kaathy Lynn, 219
Unruh, Larry, 215
Unruh, Marilyn Sue, 215

V

Vanderhayden, Helen Lucille, 160
Vanderheyden, Helen, 157-158
VanRensellaer, Carol, 278
Varner, Teri Lynn, 211
Vaught, Donna Jeanne, 203
Vaught, William Leroy, 203
Verley, James L., 208
Verley, Mary Jean, 208
Verley, Nicki Gayle, 208
Vickers, Connie, 261
Vigil, David Joe, 212

W

Waddell, Carolyn, 157-158
Waddell, Carolyn Mae, 160
Wade, Sammy, 261

Wagensen, Donald W., 160
Wagner, Donald, 157-158
Wagner, Donald G., 160
Wagner, Mr., 144-145
Wake, Kathy, 262
Waldrup, Deborah, 213
Walker, Belle, 143-144
Walker, Debra, 203
Walker, Dr. Laurence, 277-278
Walker, Howard, 203
Walker, Laurence, 284
Walker, Robert, 203
Walker, Sally Jan, 203
Walker, Vallen, 260
Wallace, Debbie, 227
Wallace, Lee, 166, 175-177
Wallace, Ruth, 166, 175
Wallace, Ted, 166, 175-176
Waller, Lisa Annette, 219
Ward, Casey, 262
Warner, Tammy, 233
Watson, Emmy, 104
Watson, Kristine, 261
Watt, Ann, 193
Watt, Dan, 193
Weaver, Alvina, 71, 177-178
Weaver, Gladys, 177
Weaver, Johnny, 178
Weaver, Mary. *See* Nelson, Mary (Weaver)
Weaver, Sam, 49, 303
Webb, Fred, 218
Webb, Kathlene Ann, 218
Weber, Clarence, 218
Weber, Sandra Lee, 218
Weeg, Brian, 265
Weese, Claudette, 195
Wegher, Laura, 261
Weir, Lester Clair, 257
Welch, Annette, 248, 251
Welch, Bobby Jo, 249, 252
Welch, George, 249
Welch, Tia, 263
Welch, Wade, 250
Welling, Linda, 252
Welling, Myra, 248
Wells, Ida, 42
Wenande, Nellie, 158, 160
Wenckus, Jeffrey Church, 203
Wenckus, Stanley B., 203
Wenger, Bobby, 193
Wenger, Sammy, 222
Wenger, Terry, 222
Wenger, Timothy James, 222
Wennade, Nellie, 240
Werger, Vikki, 227
Werner, Marguerite, 157
West, Jenny, 210

www.ingramcontent.com/pod-product-compliance
Lightning Source LLC
Chambersburg PA
CBHW062016090426
42811CB00005B/877